Bestselling Books by
Robert T. Kiyosaki & Sharon L. Lechter

Rich Dad Poor Dad
What the Rich Teach Their Kids About Money
that the Poor and Middle Class Do Not

Rich Dad's CASHFLOW Quadrant
Rich Dad's Guide to Financial Freedom

Rich Dad's Guide to Investing
What the Rich Invest In that the Poor and Middle Class Do No

Rich Dad's Rich Kid Smart Kid
Give Your Child a Financial Head Start

Rich Dad's Retire Young Retire Rich
How to Get Rich Quickly and Stay Rich Forever

Rich Dad's Prophecy
Why the Biggest Stock Market Crash in History is Still Coming...
And How You Can Prepare Yourself and Profit From it!

Rich Dad's Success Stories
Real-Life Success Stories from Real-Life People
Who Followed the Rich Dad Lessons

Rich Dad's Guide to Becoming Rich Without Cutting Up Your Credit Cards
Turn "Bad Debt" into "Good Debt"

Rich Dad's Who Took My Money?
Why Slow Investors Lose and Fast Money Wins!

Rich Dad Poor Dad for Teens
The Secrets About Money – That You Don't Learn In School!

Rich Dad's Escape from the Rat Race
How to Become a Rich Kid by Following Rich Dad's Advice

Rich Dad's Before You Quit Your Job
Ten Real-Life Lessons Every Entrepreneur Should Know
About Building a Multi-Million Dollar Business

Rich Dad's Increase Your Financial IQ
Get Smarter With Your Money
www.richdad.com

Bestselling Books by
Rich Dad's Advisors

Guide to Investing in Gold and Silver

Protect Your Financial Future

MICHAEL MALONEY

BUSINESS PLUS

NEW YORK   BOSTON

Copyright © 2008 by Michael Maloney
All rights reserved. Except as permitted under the U.S. Copyright Act of 1976, no part of this publication may be reproduced, distributed, or transmitted in any form or by any means, or stored in a database or retrieval system, without the prior written permission of the publisher.

CASHFLOW, Rich Dad, Rich Dad's Advisors, Rich Dad's Seminars, EBSI, B-I Triangle are registered trademarks of CASHFLOW Technologies, Inc.

Business Plus
Hachette Book Group
237 Park Avenue
New York, NY 10017

Visit our Web sites at www.HachetteBookGroup.com and www.richdad.com.

Business Plus is an imprint of Grand Central Publishing.
The Business Plus name and logo are trademarks of Hachette Book Group, Inc.

Printed in the United States of America

First Edition: August 2008

10 9 8 7 6 5 4 3 2

Library of Congress Cataloging-in-Publication Data (TK)

Maloney, Michael.
   Guide to investing in gold and silver : everything you need to know to profit
from precious metals now / Michael Maloney.
       p.   cm.—(Rich dad's advisors)
   ISBN-13: 978-0-446-51099-8
   ISBN-10: 0-446-51099-8
   1. Gold—Purchasing.   2. Silver—Purchasing.   3. Metals as an investment.
4. Investments.   I. Title.   II. Series.

HG293.M35   2008
332.63'28—dc22
                                                        2008023559

This publication is designed to provide general information regarding the subject matter covered. However, laws and practices often vary from state to state and are subject to change. Because each factual situation is different, specific advice should be tailored to the particular circumstances. For this reason, the reader is advised to consult with his or her own advisor regarding that individual's specific situation.

The author has taken reasonable precautions in the preparation of this book and believes the facts presented in the book are accurate as of the date it was written. However, neither the author nor the publisher assume any responsibility for any errors or omissions. The author and publisher specifically disclaim any liability resulting from the use or application of the information contained in this book, and the information is not intended to serve as legal advice related to individual situations.

For my father
Jerry Maloney
1923–1986
who instilled in me, the entrepreneurial spirit.

To

Robert & Kim Kiyosaki
Thank you for challenging everyone to be
more tomorrow than they are today.

Acknowledgments

I'd like to express my gratitude to my mother, Mae Maloney, for her encouragement, and my sister Pamela Maloney for introducing me to Robert Kiyosaki. I'd like to thank Cameron Hamza, who started me on the road to precious metals; my business partners Brent Harmes and Richard Beers for their support of this project; my editors Jake Johnson and Leila Porteous for making this book readable; Blair Singer for showing me how to build a team that wins; James Turk of GoldMoney for his insights; my friend David Morgan of Silver-Investor.com for his support and help; Kelly Ritchie, Ken McElroy, and Garrett Sutton for inspiring me; and Mona Gambetta and the Rich Dad team for making it possible. To all of you, a big huge thank you.

Contents

Foreword

by Robert Kiyosaki

I've known Mike Maloney for some time now. One thing I always hear people say about Mike is, "That guy is really smart." The reason they say this is because Mike knows a lot of facts—and I mean *a lot* of facts!

Plenty of people know facts. What sets Mike apart from the pack is his uncanny ability to connect the dots. Mike isn't just a smart person. He is a visionary who can take a large amount of information and find usable and important patterns.

The book you have in your hands covers a lot of history. Specifically it covers the history of money, or as Mike would remind us, the history of money *and* currency, which are two entirely different things. In its pages you will discover how the interaction between money and currency has steered empires throughout time. And yes, it even steers the great American empire today. You will also see how that steering affects you and your financial well-being, and you will learn how to use it to your advantage.

But Mike isn't just a historian. He's an expert. Specifically, he's an expert on gold and silver. Mike's focus on history has a very important reasoning behind it—to make you wealthy.

Mike sees the same thing I've been seeing for quite some time now: Capitalism in America is sick, on life support, and close to dead. Our problem is a toxic dollar that undermines our economic vitality.

As I write this, the price of gold is flirting with the $1,000 mark. And while I'm thrilled to see the gold I purchased for $300 only a few years back now worth over three times the price I bought it for, I'm also saddened.

You might be thinking I'm crazy to say such a thing. How could realizing such substantial returns on my money possibly disappoint me? But it's because I understand that when gold and silver prices rise like they currently are, it means that capitalism is stumbling. And when capitalism stumbles, everyday, hardworking people lose. They lose their life savings. Their house is foreclosed on. They watch their 401(k) loaded with stocks and mutual funds wither away to nothing. Meanwhile, the government bails out big corporations.

Not only that, but rising gold and silver prices also signal a rise in inflation, something Mike covers expertly and in great detail in this book. What that means for you and me is that the price of a gallon of milk keeps going up and up. It means gas prices will continue to rise. It means the basic things we need for existence get more expensive while our purchasing power diminishes. It means we are poorer every day.

For these reasons, I pray that gold doesn't reach $5,000 an ounce. Rather, I hope that the dollar goes off life support and finds a way to get back on its feet again, and I dream of a day when our government officials are once again part of a system that is of the people, for the people, and by the people, not as Mike puts it so succinctly, "Of the bankers, for the bankers, and by the bankers."

But once you've read this book, you'll know as well as I that things probably won't work out that way. And this is why Mike's work here is so important. He has made it his mission to educate as many people as possible about what he coins "The greatest coming wealth transfer in history." In this book you will learn about not just how to invest in gold and silver, but also why it is imperative for your financial well-being that you do so, and that you do so now.

In my latest book, *Rich Dad's Increase Your Financial IQ,* I write about the importance of understanding today's economy. It is not money that makes you wealthy, rather it is good information and a well-developed financial IQ. Lots of people are smart, but few have a good financial IQ.

But Mike has a tremendous financial IQ. You would do very well to heed his words and his warnings about the coming economic storm and the wealth transfer it will confer on those who have taken the time to moor their financial well-being to the rocks of gold and silver.

As Mike explains, the greatest transfer of wealth is coming soon, and gold and silver will be the major player in that wealth transfer. Whether you prepare yourself financially for this tremendous upheaval in our financial system by putting yourself in a position to grow wealth beyond your wildest imaginings is entirely in your power, and entirely up to you.

You are privileged to hold in your hand a steady compass for navigating this coming economic storm. Read it carefully, and take it to heart. I promise you'll be glad you did.

— ROBERT KIYOSAKI

Preface

I believe the greatest investment opportunity in history is knocking on your door. You can open it, or not . . . the choice is yours.

For the past 2,400 years a pattern has continually repeated in which governments debase and dilute their money supply until a point where the common psyche of the populace and the collective mind of a country begin to feel that something isn't right.

You probably feel that way right now.

As the debasement progresses, the population senses the loss of their purchasing power. Then something miraculous happens. Through the free market system, the will of the public causes gold and silver to automatically revalue. In doing so, it accounts for all the currency that was created since the last revaluation.

It's automatic, and it's natural; gold and silver have always done this, and they always will. People have an innate sense of the rarity of gold and silver. When paper money becomes too abundant, and thus loses value, man always turns back to the precious metals. When the masses come rushing back, the value (purchasing power) of gold and silver increases exponentially.

During these events there is always an enormous wealth transfer, and it is within your power to choose whether it is transferred toward you, or away from you. If you choose to have it transferred toward you, then you must first educate yourself, and second, take action.

This book is about both education and taking action. In its pages you will find both historical perspective and practical advice about how to take advantage of what I believe to be the biggest precious metals boom ever. At first you might be surprised by the amount of history I've laid out here, but I assure you there is a reason to my rhyme. For it is only by understanding our past that we can truly know the present. And presently we are faced with a very rare opportunity to increase our wealth exponentially—if we are armed with the right knowledge.

This book will equip you with all you need to become a successful precious metals investor, and will equip you with the knowledge you need to take your financial future into your own hands. Enjoy.

Introduction

One of the things Robert Kiyosaki always teaches at his live appearances is the difference between "content" and "context." *Content* is the facts, the data, the fragments of information. Whereas *context* is the way someone looks at things, their point of view, the feeling that someone has about something, and the way they approach their world. It is the big picture, or should I say, it is the ability of your mind to hold the big picture. Changing or expanding someone's context is far more powerful (and difficult) than just giving them a bunch of facts.

This book will change and expand your context—if you let it. We will explore some very "contextual" stories of how gold and silver have revalued themselves throughout history as governments abused their currencies, just as the United States is doing today. We'll talk about bubbles, manias, and panics because every investor should have some understanding of mass psychology and dynamics. After all, it is greed and fear that move the markets.

After we've explored the stories history provides for us, I will show where we are today economically, which is on the brink of economic disaster, what we will call the perfect economic storm. In the United States, the recklessness with which we spend and the poor planning our government employs has created an economic momentum that is unsustainable. As you will see, our currency (the dollar) is on its way to crashing, and this can only lead to far higher values for gold and silver. Together we will study the current state of the U.S. and global economies, and the supply and demand fundamentals of gold and silver versus the U.S. dollar.

You will also learn about two of the many natural economic cycles that repeat and repeat throughout history. One is the stock cycle, where stocks and real estate outperform gold, silver, and commodities, and then the cycle reverses and becomes a commodities cycle where gold, silver, and commodities outperform stocks and real estate. The other cycle is less known, less regular, and less frequent: the currency cycle, where societies start with quality money and then move to quantity currency and then back again.

These cycles swing like a pendulum throughout time, and they provide an economic barometer for the astute investor.

The greatest wealth can be accumulated in the shortest period of time when gold and silver revalue themselves. I believe this has already begun, and I believe that this revaluation will be staggering in its economic impact as the perfect convergence of economic cycles are brewing the perfect economic storm.

These cycles that ebb and flow throughout history are as natural as the coming of the tides. And while betting against them may be hazardous to your financial health, investing with them can bring you great wealth.

This book will unfold in four parts:

Part 1: Yesterday

In Part One of this book we will study some of the lessons history teaches us about economic cycles, paper currency, and their effect on gold and silver. I will give you examples of how gold and silver have always won out over fiat currency (a fancy term for money that is not backed by something tangible like gold or silver). I will also show you how manias and panics can change economic conditions in the blink of an eye. It is important to understand the dynamics of each because they will both play a role in what I believe will be the greatest wealth transfer in history.

Part 2: Today

In Part Two we will cover the financial shortsightedness of the United States government today, the dangerous game that the United States and China are playing with trade surpluses and deficits, and the potentially disastrous economic results. We will also see how inflation of the currency supply is not only hurting you financially, but ushering in the demise of the U.S. dollar and the economic power of the United States as we know it. Then I'll wrap it up with the fundamentals of gold and silver.

Part 3: Tomorrow

Once we are done learning what history has to teach us, and have gained an understanding of the economic conditions we face today, we will explore how that information impacts our tomorrow, our future, and our family's future. I'll show you how to not only protect yourself from the coming perfect economic storm, but to also prosper from it by applying lessons we've learned from the past and the things the present is teaching us now. As you've probably guessed, this will have something to do with wisely investing in gold and silver. That's probably why you've bought this book in the first place!

Part 4: How to Invest in Precious Metals

As you'll see, and I hope come to believe, the best possible investments given today's economic environment are gold and silver. In the last section of this book, I'll give you some good sound advice on the ins and outs of precious metals investing.

For many, precious metal investing is an alien environment with a reputation for being populated by a bunch of kooks and conspiracy theorists—and it is to some extent. But don't let a few bad apples ruin the whole barrel. As you'll see, history is well on the side of these "kooks" who love their gold and silver. Part Four will demystify the concept of investing in gold and silver. Investing in these metals is not only relatively easy, but it is also very safe.

Above all, as I mentioned earlier, this book is about changing your context.

The reason precious metals investing seems so alien and out there is because there are very powerful and wealthy companies and individuals that have a vested interest in maintaining the status quo. They want you to play their game. What I mean by that is that they benefit financially by making sure you keep *your* money in *their* hands.

Precious metals essentially eliminate the middleman. They are the only financial assets that do not have to be "in" the financial system. No financial advisor gets a bonus for pushing you into them like when you buy stocks and mutual funds. One of the reasons I'm proud to be part of the Rich Dad family is because it makes a point of exposing the game that the financial industry plays with your money. In the process they stress the importance of increasing your financial IQ by reading books like this one and others in the Rich Dad series. Once you are equipped with knowledge, you can recognize how the system plays you, and you can take control of your own financial future.

Playing their game is all fine and dandy—if you don't care to increase your financial intelligence or to invest wisely. But when the whole system comes crashing down, don't say I didn't warn you. After you've finished reading this book, if I've done my job correctly, you will never be able to look at our financial institutions the same way. Your context will be changed, and a new horizon as bright as the morning sun will be before you.

I'll see you on the other side.

Part 1

Yesterday

Chapter 1

The Battle of the Ages

Throughout the history of civilizations an epic battle has always been waged. It is an unseen battle, unknown by most of the people it affects. Yet, all feel the effects of this battle in their daily lives. Whether it be at the supermarket when you notice that a gallon of milk is a dollar more than it was last time, or when you get your heating bill and it has unexpectedly jumped by $50, you are feeling the effects of this hidden battle.

This battle is between currency and money, and it is truly a battle of the ages.

Most often this battle takes place between gold and silver, and currencies that supposedly represent the value of gold and silver. Inevitably people always think that currency will win. They have the same blind faith every time, but in the end, gold and silver always revalue themselves and they always win.

To understand how gold and silver periodically revalue, you first need to know the differences between money and currency.

Throughout the ages many things have been currency. Livestock, grains, spices, shells, beads, and paper have all been forms of currency, but only two things have been money. You guessed it: gold and silver.

Currency

A lot of people think currency is money. For instance, when someone gives you some cash, you presumably think of it as money. It is not. Cash is simply a currency, a medium of exchange that you can use to purchase something that has value, what we would call an asset.

As Robert Kiyosaki explains in *Rich Dad's Increase Your Financial IQ*, currency is derived from the word current. A current must keep moving or else it will die (think electricity). A currency does not store value in and of itself. Rather, it is a medium whereby you can transfer value from one asset to another.

Money

Money, unlike currency, has value within itself. Money is always a currency, in that it can be used to purchase other items that have value, but as we've just learned, currency is not always money because it doesn't have value in and of itself. If you are having a hard time grasping this, just think about a hundred-dollar bill. Do you think that paper is worth $100?

The answer is, of course, no. That paper simply represents value that is stored somewhere else—or at least it used to be before our money became currency. Later we will study the history of our currency and the gold standard, but for now all you need to know is that the U.S. dollar is backed by nothing other than hot air, or what is commonly referred to as "the good faith and credit of the United States." In short, our government has the ability to, and has been, creating money at will without anything to back it up. You might call this counterfeiting; the government calls it fiscal policy. The whole thing is what we refer to as fiat currency.

Fiat Currency

A fiat is an arbitrary decree, order, or pronouncement given by a person, group, or body with the absolute authority to enforce it. A currency that derives its value from declaratory fiat or an authoritative order of the government is by definition a fiat currency. All currencies in use today are fiat currencies.

For the rest of this book I will use these proper definitions. At first it will sound strange to you, but it will only serve to highlight, and bring greater understanding of, the differences between currency and money. Hopefully, by the end of the book you will see that it is the general public's lack of understanding concerning this difference between currency and money that has created what I believe will be the greatest wealth accumulation opportunity in history. What you will learn about currency and money in this book is knowledge that probably 99 percent of the population has no clue about or desire to learn. So congratulations, you will be way ahead of the game.

Inflation

When I talk about inflation or deflation I'm talking about the expansion or contraction of the currency supply. The symptom of monetary inflation or deflation is rising or falling prices, which I will sometimes refer to as price inflation or price deflation. Regardless, one thing is for sure. With inflation everything gets more valuable except currency.

Adventures in Currency Creation

Fiat currencies don't usually start out that way, and those rare cases when they have were very short-lived. Societies usually start with high value commodity money such as gold and silver. Gradually, the government hoodwinks the population into accepting fiat currency by issuing paper demand notes that are redeemable in precious metals. These demand notes (currency) are really just "certificates of deposit," "receipts," or "claim checks" on the real money that is in the vault. I would venture to say that many Americans think this is how the U.S. dollar works today.

Once a government has introduced a paper currency, they then expand the currency supply through deficit spending, printing even more of the currency to cover that spending, and through credit creation based on fractional reserve banking (something we'll cover later on). Then, usually due to war or some other national emergency, like foreign governments or the local population trying to redeem their demand notes (bank runs), the government will suspend redemption rights because they don't have enough gold and silver to cover all of the paper they have printed, and poof! You have a fiat currency.

Here's the dirty little secret: Fiat currency is designed to lose value. Its very purpose is to confiscate your wealth and transfer it to the government. Each time the government prints a new dollar and spends it, the government gets the full purchasing power of that dollar. But where did that purchasing power come from? It was secretly stolen from the dollars you hold. As each new dollar enters circulation it devalues all the other dollars in existence because there are now more dollars chasing the same amount of goods and services. This causes prices to rise. It is the insidious stealth tax known as inflation, robbing you of your wealth like a thief in the night.

Throughout the centuries, gold and silver have battled it out with fiat currency, and the precious metals have always won. Gold and silver revalue themselves automatically through the free market system, balancing themselves against the fiat currency in the process. This is a pattern that has been repeating and repeating since the first great currency crash in Athens in 407 B.C. Whenever an investor detects the beginning of one of these battles, the opportunities (according to history) to accumulate great wealth in a very short period of time are enormous.

It always seems to start the same way. Energy builds as the currency supply is expanded, and then, through natural human instincts, the coming crash is felt by the masses, and suddenly, in an explosive move and in a relatively short amount of time, gold and silver will revalue themselves to account for the currency that has been created in the meantime, and then some. If you see the writing on the wall and then take action before the masses do, your purchasing power will grow exponentially as gold and silver grow in value relative to an inflated currency. If you don't, you're in for a wipeout.

These heavyweight bouts between fiat currency and gold and silver can end one of two ways:

1. A technical decision, where the fiat currency becomes an asset backed by gold or silver again.

Or:

2. A knockout blow that is the death of the fiat currency.

Either way, gold and silver are always declared the victors. They are always the reigning heavyweight champions of the world. But you don't have to take my word for it. Let's see what history has to say.

It's All Greek to Me

Winston Churchill once said, "The farther backward you can look, the farther forward you are likely to see." So in the spirit of Churchill, we are going to look back . . . way back to the time of the Greeks.

Gold and silver have been the predominant currency for 4,500 years, but they became money in Lydia, in about 680 B.C. when they were minted into coins of equal weight in order to make trade easier and smoother. But it was when coinage first made its appearance in Athens that it truly flourished. Athens was the world's first democracy. They had the world's first free-market system and working tax system. This made possible those amazing architectural public works like the Parthenon.

Indeed for many years the Athens star shone brightly. If you've studied your history, then you know they are considered one of the great civilizations of all time. You'll also know that their civilization fell a long time ago. So what happened? Why did such a great and powerful civilization like Athens fall? The answer lies in the same pattern we can see time and time again throughout history: too much greed leading to too much war.

Athens flourished under their new monetary system. Then they became involved in a war that turned out to be much longer and far more costly than they anticipated (sound familiar?). After twenty-two years of war, their resources waning and most of their money spent, the Athenians came up with a very clever way to continue funding the war. They began to debase their money in an attempt to soldier on. In a stroke of genius the Athenians discovered that if you take in 1,000 coins in taxes and mix 50 percent copper in with your gold and silver you can then spend 2,000 coins! Does this sound familiar to you? It should . . . it's called deficit spending, and our government does it every second of every day.

This was the first time in history that gold or silver had a price outside itself. Before the Athenians' bright idea, everything that you could buy was priced in a weight of gold or silver. Now, for the first time, there was official government currency that was not gold and silver, but rather a mixture of gold or silver and copper. You could buy gold and silver with it, but the currency supply was no longer gold and silver in and of themselves.

Over the next two years their beautiful money became nothing more than currency, and as a consequence it became practically worthless. But obviously, once the public woke up to the debasement, anyone who had held on to the old pure gold and silver coins saw their purchasing power increase dramatically.

Within a couple of years the war that had started the whole process had been lost. Athens would never again enjoy the glory they once knew, and they eventually became nothing more than a province of the next great power, Rome.

And the very first regional heavyweight bout between currency and money goes to the "real money," as gold and silver are crowned the "Heavyweight Champions of Athens".

Rome Is Burning

Rome supplanted the Greek empire as the dominant power of its day, and during its centuries of dominance, the Romans had ample time to perfect the art of currency debasement. Just as with every empire in history, Rome never learned from the mistakes of past empires, and therefore they were doomed to repeat them.

Over 750 years, various leaders inflated the Roman currency supply by debasing the coinage to pay for war, which would lead to staggering price inflation. Coins were made smaller, or a small portion of the edge of gold coins would be clipped off as a tax when entering a government building. These clippings would then be melted down to make more coins. And of course, just as the Greeks did, they too mixed lesser metals such as copper into their gold and silver. And last but not least, they invented the not so subtle art of revaluation, meaning they simply minted the same coins but with a higher face value on them.

By the time Diocletian ascended to the throne in A.D. 284, the Roman coins were nothing more than tin-plated copper or bronze, and inflation (and the Roman populace) was raging.

In 301, Diocletian issued his infamous Edict of Prices, which imposed the death penalty on anyone selling goods for more than the government-mandated price and also froze wages. To Diocletian's surprise, however, prices just kept rising. Merchants could no longer sell their wares at a profit, so they closed up shop. People either left their chosen careers to seek one where wages weren't fixed, or just gave up and accepted welfare from the state. Oh yeah, the Romans invented welfare. Rome had a population of about one million, and at this period of time, the government was doling out free wheat to approximately 200,000 citizens. That equaled out to 20 percent of the population on welfare.

Because the economy was so poor, Diocletian adopted a guns and butter policy, putting people to work by hiring thousands of new soldiers and funding numerous public works projects. This effectively doubled the size of the government and the military, and probably increased deficit spending by many multiples.

When you add the cost of paying all these troops to the swelling masses of the unemployed poor receiving welfare and the rising costs of new public works projects, the numbers were staggering. Deficit spending went into overdrive. When he ran short of funds, Diocletian simply minted vast quantities of new copper and bronze coins and began, once again, debasing the gold and silver coins.

All this resulted in the world's first documented hyperinflation. In Diocletian's Edict of Prices (a very well preserved copy of which was unearthed in 1970), a pound of gold was worth 50,000 denari in the year A.D. 301, but by mid-century was worth 2.12 billion denari. That means the price of gold rose 42,400 times in fifty or so years. This resulted in all currency-based trade coming to a virtual standstill, and the economic system reverted to a barter system.

To put this in perspective, fifty years ago the price of gold was $35 per ounce in the United States. If it rose 42,400 times, the price today would be just under $1.5 million per ounce. In terms of purchasing power, that means if an average new car sold for about $2,000 fifty years ago, which they did, the average car today would sell for $85 million.

This signaled the second great victory for gold and silver over fiat currency in history. So there you go, gold and silver are now 2 and 0.

In the end it was currency debasement and pure deficit spending to fund the military, public works, social programs, and war that brought down the Roman Empire. Just as with every empire throughout history, it thought it was immune to the laws of economics.

As you will see, debasing the currency to pay for public works, social programs, and war is a pattern that repeats throughout history. It is a pattern that always ends badly.

Chapter 2

The Wealth of Nations

In studying monetary history to identify cycles, it is necessary to examine both sides of the coin so to speak. The temptation is for people to blame all their woes on their government. Certainly governments are often at fault when it comes to inflation through fiat monetary policy, but one must never forget that in the end we are ultimately the ones who consent to our government's rule. History is full of examples of greed leading a populace to do incredibly stupid things. Indeed, we don't need government to ruin our economy. We can get by just fine by ourselves, thank you.

The best example I can think of is the tulip mania of 1637.

A Tulip Is Still a Tulip . . .

In order to understand the absurdity of this moment in history I'm about to share with you, you simply have to ask yourself: *Would I pay $1.8 million for a tulip bulb?* If the answer to that question is yes, then please put this book down and get some professional help. Otherwise, read on and see just how crazy the public can become.

Everyone thinks of tulips when they think of Holland. Then they think of beer. What many people don't know is that tulips are not indigenous to

Holland. They were imported. In 1593 the first tulip bulbs were brought from Turkey to Holland. They quickly became a status symbol for royalty and the wealthy. This developed into a mania, and soon a tulip exchange was established in Amsterdam.

Very quickly this mania turned into an economic bubble. You may find this comical; in 1636 a single tulip bulb of the Viceroy variety was traded for the following: 2 lasts (a last is 4,000 pounds) of wheat, 4 lasts of rye, 4 fat oxen, 8 fat swine, 12 fat sheep, 2 hogsheads (140 gallon wooden barrel) of wine, 4 tons of beer, 2 tons of butter, 1,000 pounds of cheese, 1 bed, 1 suit of clothes, and 1 silver goblet.

At its very peak in 1637 a single bulb of the Semper Augustus variety was sold for 6,000 florins. The average yearly wage in Holland at the time was 150 florins. That means that tulip bulbs were selling for 40 times the average Hollander's annual income. To put that into perspective, let's assume the average U.S. salary is $45,000. That means that a tulip bulb in today's terms would cost you $1.8 million.

Soon people began to realize how absolutely crazy the situation had become, and the smart money (if you can call anyone involved in this mania smart) began to sell. Within weeks tulip bulb prices fell to their real value, which was several tulip bulbs for just *one* florin.

The financial devastation that swept across northern Europe as a result of this market crash lasted for decades.

John Law and Central Banking

Another great example of a society replacing its money with an ever inflating currency supply is the story of John Law. John Law's life was a true rollercoaster ride of epic proportions.

Born the son of a Scottish goldsmith and banker, John Law was a bright boy with high mathematical aptitude. He grew up to be quite a gambler and ladies' man, and lost most of his family fortune in the course of his exploits. At one point, he got into a fight over a woman and his opponent challenged him to a duel. He shot his opponent dead, was arrested, tried, and sentenced to hang. Being the knave that he was, Law escaped from prison and fled to France.

Meanwhile, Louis XIV was running France deeply into debt due to war mongering and his lavish lifestyle. John Law, who was now living in Paris, became a gambling buddy with the Duke d'Orleans, and it was at about this time that Law published an economic paper promoting the benefits of paper currency.

When Louis XIV died, his successor, Louis XV was only eleven years old. The Duke d'Orleans was placed as regent (temporary king), and to his horror he found out that France was so deep in debt that taxes didn't even cover the interest payments on that debt. Law, sensing opportunity, showed up at the royal court with two papers for his friend blaming the problems of France on insufficient currency and expounding the virtues of paper currency. On May 15, 1716, John Law was given a bank (Banque Générale) and the right to issue paper currency, and there began Europe's foray into paper currency.

The slightly increased currency supply brought a new vitality to the economy, and John Law was hailed as a financial genius. As a reward the Duke d'Orleans granted Law the rights to all trade from France's Louisiana Territory in America. The Louisiana Territory was a huge area comprising about 30 percent of what is now the United States, stretching from Canada to the mouth of the Mississippi River.

At that time, it was believed that Louisiana was rich in gold, and John Law's new Mississippi Company, with the exclusive rights to trade from this territory, quickly became the richest company in France. John Law wasted no time capitalizing on the public's confidence in his company's prospects and issued 200,000 company shares. Shortly after that the share price exploded, rising by more than 30 times in a period of months. Just imagine, in a few short years, Law went from a gambling addict and penniless murderer to one of the most powerful financial figures in Europe.

Again, Law was rewarded. This time the Duke bestowed upon him and his companies a monopoly on the sale of tobacco, the sole right to refine and coin silver and gold, and he made Law's bank the Banque Royale. Law was now at the helm of France's central bank.

Now that his bank was the royal bank of France it meant that the government backed his new paper notes, just as our government backs the Federal Reserve's paper notes. And since everything was going so well, the Duke asked John Law to issue even more notes, and Law, agreeing that there is no such thing as too much of a good thing, obliged. The government spent foolishly and recklessly while Law was pacified with gifts, honors, and titles.

Yes, things were going quite well. So well, in fact, that the Duke thought that if this much currency brought so much prosperity, then twice as much would be even better. Just a couple of years earlier the government couldn't even pay the interest on its debt, and now, not only had it paid off its debt, but it could also spend as much currency as it wanted. All it had to do was print it.

As a reward for Law's service to France, the Duke passed an edict granting the Mississippi Company the exclusive right to trade in the East Indies, China, and the South Seas. Upon hearing this news, Law decided to issue 50,000 new shares of the Mississippi Company. When he made the new stock offer, more than 300,000 applications were made for the new shares. Among them were dukes, marquises, counts, and duchesses, all waiting to get their shares. Law's solution to the problem was to issue 300,000 shares instead of the 50,000 he was originally planning, a 500 percent increase in the total number of shares.

Paris was booming due to the rampant stock speculation and the increased currency supply. All the shops were full, there was an abundance of new luxury goods, and the streets were bustling. As Charles Mackay puts it in his book *Extraordinary Popular Delusions and the Madness of Crowds*, "New houses were built in every direction, and an illusory prosperity shone over the land, and so dazzled the eyes of the whole nation, that none could see the dark cloud on the horizon announcing the storm that was too rapidly approaching."

Soon, however, problems started to crop up. Due to the inflation of the currency supply, prices started to skyrocket. Real estate values and rents, for instance, increased 20-fold.

Law also began to feel the effects of the rampant inflation he had helped create. With the next stock issue of the Mississippi Company, Law offended the Prince de Conti when he refused to issue him shares at the price the royal wanted. Furious, the Prince sent three wagons to the bank to cash in all of his paper currency and Mississippi stock. He was paid with three wagonloads-ful of gold and silver coin. The Duke d'Orleans, however, was incensed and demanded the Prince return the coin to the bank. Fearing that he'd never be able to set foot in Paris again, the Prince returned two of the three wagonloads.

This was a wake-up call to the public, and the "smart money" began to exit fast. People started converting their notes to coin, and bought anything of transportable value. Jewelry, silverware, gemstones, and coin were bought and sent abroad or hoarded.

In order to stop the bleeding, in February of 1720 the banks discontinued note redemption for gold and silver, and it was declared illegal to use gold or silver coin in payment. Buying jewelry, precious stones, or silverware was also outlawed. Rewards were offered of 50 percent of any gold or silver confiscated from those found in possession of such goods (payable in banknotes of course). The borders were closed and carriages searched. The prisons filled and heads rolled, literally.

Finally, the financial crisis came to a head. On May 27, the banks were closed and Law was dismissed from the ministry. Banknotes were devalued by 50 percent, and on June 10 the banks reopened and resumed redemption of the notes for gold at the new value. When the gold ran out, people were paid in silver. When the silver ran out, people were paid in copper. As you can imagine, the frenzy to convert paper back to coin was so intense that near riot conditions ensued. Gold and silver had delivered a knockout blow.

By then John Law was now the most reviled man in France. In a matter of months he went from arguably the most powerful and influential force in society back to the nobody he was before. Law fled to Venice where he resumed his life as a gambler, lamenting, "Last year I was the richest individual who ever lived. Today I have nothing, not even enough to keep alive." He died broke, in Venice, in 1729.

The collapse of the Mississippi Company and Law's fiat currency system plunged France and most of Europe into a horrible depression, which lasted for decades. But what astounds me most is that this all transpired in just four short years.

The Weimar Republic—A Painful Lesson Learned

By now you've learned the kind of damage fiat currency can cause. Now let's look at another example and identify the silver lining (no pun intended), and how such extreme situations can actually present opportunities to acquire vast wealth.

At the beginning of World War I, Germany went off the gold standard and suspended the right of its citizens to redeem their currency (the mark) for gold and silver. Like all wars, World War I was a war of and by the printing press. The number of marks in circulation in Germany quadrupled during the war. Prices, however, had not kept up with the inflation of the currency supply. So the effects of this inflation were not felt.

The reason for this peculiar phenomenon was because in times of uncertainty people tend to save every penny. World War I was definitely a time of uncertainty. So even though the German government was pumping tons of currency into the system, no one was spending it—yet. But by war's end, confidence flooded back along with the currency that had been on the sidelines, and the ravaging effects worked their way through the country as prices rose to catch up with the previous monetary inflation.

Just before the end of the war, the exchange rate between gold and the mark was about 100 marks per ounce. But by 1920 it was fluctuating between 1,000 and 2,000 marks per ounce. Retail prices shortly followed suit, rising by 10 to 20 times. Anyone who still had the savings they had accumulated during the war was bewildered when they found it could only buy 10 percent or less of what it could just a year or two earlier.

Then, all through the rest of 1920 and the first half of 1921, inflation slowed, and on the surface the future was beginning to look a little brighter. The economy was recovering, business and industrial production was up. But now there were war reparations to pay, so the government never stopped printing currency. In the summer of 1921 prices started rising again and by July of 1922 prices had risen another 700 percent.

This was the breaking point. And what broke was people's confidence in their economy and their currency. Having watched the purchasing power of their savings fall by 90 percent in 1919, they knew better this time around. They were smarter; they had been here before.

All at once, the entire country's attitude toward currency changed. People knew that if they held on to their currency for any period of time they'd get burned . . . the rising prices would wipe out their purchasing power. Suddenly everybody started to spend their currency as soon as they got it. The currency became a hot potato, and no one wanted to hang on to it for a second.

After the war, Germany made the first reparations payment to France with most of its gold and made up the balance with iron, coal, wood, and other materials, but it simply didn't have the resources to meet its second payment. France thought Germany was just trying to weasel its way out of paying. So, in January of 1923, France and Belgium invaded and occupied the Ruhr (the industrial heartland of Germany). The invading troops took over the iron and steel factories, coal mines and railways.

In response, the German Weimar government adopted a policy of passive resistance and noncooperation, paying the factories' workers, all 2 million of them, not to work. This was the last nail in the German mark's coffin.

Meanwhile, the government put its printing presses into overdrive. According to the front page of the *New York Times*, February 9, 1923, Germany had thirty-three printing plants that were belching out 45 billion marks every day! By November it was 500 *quadrillion* a day (yes, that's a real number).

The German public's confidence, however, was falling faster than the government could print the new currency. The government was caught in a downward economic spiral. A point of no return had been passed. No matter how many marks the government printed, the value fell quicker than the new currency could enter into circulation. So the government had no choice but to keep printing more and more and more.

By late October and early November 1923, the German financial system was breaking down. A pair of shoes that cost 12 marks before the war now cost 30 *trillion* marks. A loaf of bread went from half a mark to 200 *billion* marks. A single egg went from 0.08 mark to 80 *billion* marks. The German stock market went from 88 points at the end of the war to 26,890,000,000, but its *purchasing* value had fallen by more than 97 percent.

Only gold and silver outpaced inflation. The price of gold had gone from around 100 marks to 87 trillion marks per ounce, an 87 trillion percent increase in price. But it is not price, but value, that matters, and the purchasing power of gold and silver had gone up exponentially.

When Germany's hyperinflation finally came to an end on November 15, 1923, the currency supply had grown from 29.2 billion marks at the beginning of 1919 to 497 quintillion marks, an increase of the currency supply of more than 17 billion times. The total value of the currency supply, however, had dropped 97.7 percent against gold.

The poor were so before the crisis, so they were affected the least. The

Chart 1. Price of 1 Ounce of Gold in German Marks from 1914–1923

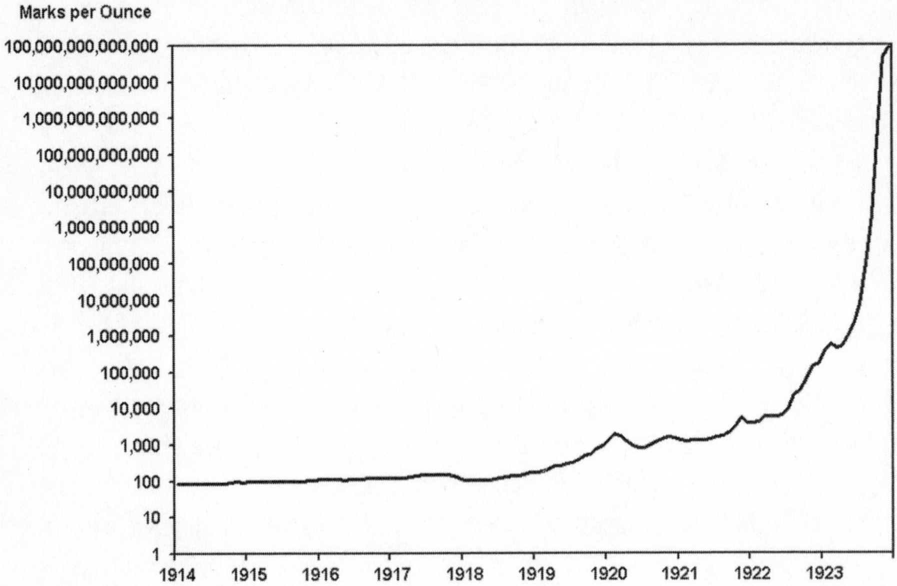

Marks per Ounce

Source: Bernd Widdig, Culture and Inflation in Weimar Germany (Univ. of CalPress, 2001)

rich, at least the smart ones, got a whole lot richer. But it was the middle class that was hurt the most. In fact, it was all but obliterated.

But there were a few exceptions. There were a few who had the right qualities and cunning to take advantage of the economic environment. They were shrewd, adept, and nimble, but most of all, adaptable. Those who could quickly adapt to a world they had never seen before, a world turned upside down, prospered. It didn't matter what class they came from, poor or middle class, if they could adapt, and adapt well, they could become wealthy in a matter of months.

At this time, an entire city block of commercial real estate in downtown Berlin could be purchased for just 25 ounces of gold ($500). The reason for this is that those who held their wealth in the form of currency became poorer and poorer as they watched their purchasing power destroyed by the government. On the flip side, those who held their wealth in the form of gold watched their purchasing power increase exponentially as they became wealthy by comparison.

Here is the important lesson: During financial upheaval, a bubble pop-ping, a market crash, a depression, or a currency crisis such as this one, wealth is not destroyed. It is merely transferred. During the Weimar hyperinflation, gold and silver didn't just win, but smashed their opponent into the ground, by delivering yet another devastating knockout blow to fiat currency. Thus, those who held on to real money, instead of currency, reaped the rewards many times over.

Chapter 3
Old Glory

I hope by now you're beginning to see a pattern develop. In all the examples I've shown you so far (and there are plenty more), the pattern is the same:

1. A sovereign state starts out with good money (i.e., money that is gold or silver, or backed fully by gold and silver).
2. As it develops economically and socially, it begins to take on more and more economic burdens, adding layer upon layer of public works and social programs.
3. As its economic affluence grows so does its political influence, and it increases expenditures to fund a massive military.
4. Eventually it puts its military to use, and expenditures explode.
5. To fund the war, the costliest of mankind's endeavors, it steals the wealth of its people by replacing their money with currency that can be created in unlimited quantities. It does this either at the outbreak of the war (as in the case of World War I), during the war or wars (as in the cases of Athens and Rome), or as a perceived solution to the economic ravages of previous wars (as in the case of John Law's France).

6. Finally, the wealth transfer caused by expansion of the currency supply is felt by the population as severe consumer price inflation, triggering a loss of faith in the currency.
7. An en masse movement out of the currency into precious metals and other tangible assets takes place, the currency collapses, and massive wealth is transferred to those who had enough foresight to accumulate gold and silver early on.

But surely something like this can't happen to the United States, you might say. We are, after all, the greatest country in the history of the world. Beyond that we aren't an empire. We don't conquer nations; we spread democracy.

We may not be an empire in the traditional sense of the word, but when it comes to economic issues, we operate like one in many ways. This is why I believe that not only will the United States decline and see its dollar crash; it's already on its way. Let's take a trip down memory lane and see how the United States got to this point in history.

Dread the Fed, the Golden Rule Is Dead

The beginning of the end for the United States economy started with the inception of the Federal Reserve. The Fed, as it's called, is a private bank, separate from the U.S. government, with the power to dictate our country's fiscal policy. Since the Fed's formation, the U.S. dollar has become nothing but currency.

From roughly 1871 to 1914, when World War I began, most of the developed world operated under what is referred to as the classical gold standard, meaning most of the world's currencies were pegged to gold. This meant that they were also pegged to each other. Businesspeople could make plans and projections far into the future, ship goods, start businesses, and invest in foreign lands, and they always knew exactly what the exchange rate would be.

On average over the period when the developed world was on the classical gold standard, there was *no* inflation . . . none, zero zip, nada. Sure, there were a few booms and busts, inflations and deflations. But from the beginning of the classical gold standard to the end, it averaged out as a zero sum game. The reason? Gold: the great equalizer.

Here's why: When countries experienced economic booms, they imported more goods. The imported goods were paid for with gold, so gold flowed out. As gold flowed out of the countries, their currency supplies contracted (that is monetary deflation). This caused these economies to slow down and the demand for imports to fall. As the economy slowed, prices fell, making these countries' goods more attractive to foreign buyers. And as exports rose to meet foreign demand, gold flowed back into that country. Then the process started all over again, the value of currency—based on gold—always moving up and down, in a narrow range, maintaining the equilibrium.

During the classical gold standard our currency was real, verifiable money, meaning that there was actual gold and silver in the Treasury backing it up. The currency was just a receipt for the money. Then, in stepped the Fed, one of the most notorious and misunderstood institutions in the history of the United States.

The difficulty with the Fed is that there's a lot of information out there, which is one reason why it's so controversial. There are two very polarized camps when it comes to the Fed. On one end you have the government, which trusts it to regulate the U.S. economy. On the other end, you have the conspiracy theorists, who believe, in no uncertain terms, that the Fed will eventually bring about the collapse of the U.S. economy.

Well, I'm here to tell you these "crackpots" are not as crazy as they may seem. For one thing, the Federal Reserve is *not* a government agency. It is a privately owned bank that has stockholders to whom it pays dividends. It has the power to actually *create* currency from nothing, and it is shielded from audits and congressional oversight. As former senator and presidential contender Barry Goldwater pointed out, "The accounts of the Federal Reserve System have never been audited. It operates outside the control of Congress and manipulates the credit of the United States."

Not So Humble Beginnings

Famed Austrian School economist Murray N. Rothbard, the vice president of the Ludwig von Mises Institute, distinguished professor of economics, and author of twenty-six books, opens his book *The Case Against the Fed* with the following:

By far the most secret and least accountable operation of the federal government is not, as one might expect, the CIA, DIA, or some other super-secret intelligence agency. The CIA and other intelligence operations are under control of Congress. They are accountable: a Congressional committee supervises these operations, controls their budgets, and is informed of their covert activities.

The Federal Reserve, however, is accountable to no one; it has no budget; it is subject to no audit; and no Congressional committee knows of, or can truly supervise, its operations. The Federal Reserve, virtually in total control of the nation's monetary system, is accountable to nobody.

Here's how it all got started. You might call this the not so humble beginning.

In 1907 there was a banking and stock market panic in the U.S., aptly called the Panic of 1907. It was widely believed that the big New York banks known as the Money Trust had been causing crashes, and then capitalizing on them by buying up stocks from rattled investors and selling them for tremendous profit just days or weeks later. The Panic of 1907 was a particularly devastating one for the U.S. economy, and there was an outcry by the general public for the government to do something.

In 1908 Congress created the National Monetary Commission to research the situation, and to recommend banking reforms that would prevent such panics, as well as to investigate the Money Trust. Senator Nelson Aldrich was appointed chairman, and immediately set out for Europe, spending two years and $300,000 (that's $6 million adjusted for inflation) to consult with the private central bankers of England, France, and Germany.

Upon his return, Senator Aldrich decided to take some time off and organized a duck hunt with some friends. The friends he invited on vacation with him were the who's who of U.S. economic power, the very New York bankers he was supposed to be investigating: Paul Warburg (Kuhn, Loeb & Company), Abraham Pete Andrew (assistant secretary of the treasury), Frank Vanderlip (president of the Rockefeller-lead National City Bank of New York), Henry P. Davison (senior partner at J. P. Morgan), Charles D. Norton (president of the Morgan-led First National Bank of New York), and Benjamin

Strong (head of J. P. Morgan Bankers Trust, and to become the first Federal Reserve head).

It is estimated that these men represented one quarter of the world's wealth. The retreat took place on a little island off the coast of Georgia called Jekyll Island. But there wasn't much duck hunting; instead Aldrich and his distinguished guests spent nine days around a table hatching a plan that eventually created the Federal Reserve.

Here is what some of the attendees had to say about that meeting:

Picture a party of the nation's greatest bankers stealing out of New York on a private railroad car under cover of darkness, stealthily hieing hundreds of miles South, embarking on a mysterious launch, sneaking on to an island deserted by all but a few servants, living there a full week under such rigid secrecy that the names of not one of them was once mentioned lest the servants learn the identity and disclose to the world this strangest, most secret expedition in the history of American finance.

I am not romancing. I am giving to the world, for the first time, the real story of how the famous Aldrich currency report, the foundation of our new currency system, was written.

B. C. Forbes, Forbes magazine, 1916

The results of the conference were entirely confidential. Even the fact there had been a meeting was not permitted to become public. Though eighteen years have since gone by, I do not feel free to give a description of this most interesting conference concerning which Senator Aldrich pledged all participants to secrecy.

Paul Warburg, The Federal Reserve System:
Its Origin and Growth

There was an occasion, near the close of 1910, when I was as secretive, indeed, as furtive, as any conspirator. I do not feel it is any exaggeration to speak of our secret expedition to Jekyll Island as the occasion of the actual conception of what eventually became the Federal Reserve System. We were told to leave our last names behind us. . . . We were instructed to come one at a time and as unobtrusively as possible to the railroad terminal on the New Jersey littoral of the Hudson, where Senator Aldrich's private car would be in readiness. . . . The servants and train crew may have known the identities of one or two of us, but they did not know all, and it was the names of all printed together that would have made our mysterious journey significant in Washington, in Wall Street, even in London. Discovery, we knew, simply must not happen, or else all our time and effort would be wasted. If it were to be exposed publicly that our particular group had got together and written a banking bill, that bill would have no chance whatever of passage by Congress.

Frank Vanderlip, quoted in
The Saturday Evening Post, February 9, 1935

Secrecy was so important to the attendees of this summit because Aldrich, as the chairman of the National Monetary Commission, was charged with investigating banking practices and recommending reforms after the Panic of 1907, not to conspire with the bankers on a remote island. So the bankers who were under investigation for needed reforms got together with the chairman of the congressional investigating committee (the guy that was supposed to investigate the suspects) at a secret meeting on an isolated island and concocted a bill, the Aldrich Plan, for a private central bank that they (the suspects) would own. When the bill was presented to Congress, the debates raged.

In one debate, Congressman Charles Lindbergh was quoted as saying, "Our financial system is a false one and a huge burden on the people. I have alleged that there is a Money Trust. The Aldrich Plan is a scheme plainly in the interest of the Trust. Why does the Money Trust press so hard for the Aldrich Plan now, before the people know what the Money Trust has been doing?"

But the Aldrich Plan never came to a vote in Congress, because it was a Republican-backed bill and the Republicans lost control of the House in 1910, and the Senate in 1912.

Not accepting defeat, the bankers essentially took the Aldrich Plan and changed a few details. In 1913 a nearly identical bill, called the Federal Reserve Act, was presented to Congress.

Again the debates raged. Many saw this bill for what it was: a prettied-up version of the Aldrich Plan. But on December 22, 1913, Congress gave up its right to coin money and regulate the value thereof, which was given it by the Constitution, and passed that right to a private corporation, the Federal Reserve.

The Fed and the Death of the Dollar— Fractional Reserve Banking

Since the Fed opened for business in 1914, the currency of the United States (the U.S. dollar) has been borrowed into existence from a private bank (the Fed). The reason I say "borrowed" into existence is because every single dollar the Fed has ever created is owed back to that bank, with interest. The Fed creates all currency, not the U.S. government, and lends it out to the U.S. government and private institutions—with interest. Now you may be asking yourself, "If we pay back all the currency that was borrowed into existence, but we still owe the interest, where do we get the currency to pay the interest?" Answer: We have to borrow it into existence. This is one reason why the national debt keeps expanding. It can never be paid off. It is mathematically impossible.

But even more disconcerting is the way the Federal Reserve creates currency:

1. It makes loans to the government or banking system by writing a bad check.
2. It buys something with a bad check.

In the Fed's own words, published in a 1977 paper called *Putting It Simply*, "When you or I write a check there must be sufficient funds in our account to cover the check, but when the Federal Reserve writes a check there is no bank deposit on which that check is drawn. When the Federal Reserve writes a check, it is creating money." Of course, as you know by now, I would beg to differ. They are creating currency, not money.

And once those newly created dollars are deposited in the banks, the banks get to employ the miracle of *fractional reserve banking*.

Here is fractional reserve banking in a nutshell. All banks have a reserve requirement, meaning they must keep a certain amount of currency on hand for withdrawals and such. If the reserve requirement set by the Fed is 10 percent the bank must keep 10 percent of the currency deposited on hand just in case someone wants to make a withdrawal; however, they are allowed to loan out the other 90 percent of those deposits.

Here's the kicker. They don't actually loan out the currency that's in the accounts. Instead they create new fiat dollars out of nothing and then loan them out, which means they too are "borrowed" into existence. In other words, when you deposit $1,000, the bank can create 900 brand-new credit dollars with nothing but a book entry, and then loan them out with interest.

Then, if those brand-new loaned dollars are deposited in a checking account, the bank is allowed to create another 90 percent of the value of those deposits, and then another 90 percent of that. Then the process is repeated, and round and round it goes.

Coincidentally, the same year that the Federal Reserve Act was passed, there was also an amendment added to the Constitution: the Sixteenth, which created the dreaded income tax.

Before 1913 there was no income tax. The entire government was paid for by tariffs (duties on imports) and excise tax (taxes on things like alcohol, cigarettes, and gas). These taxes, and only these taxes, generated enough income for the government to operate. However, because it didn't generate enough income to pay the interest due to the Federal Reserve, the income tax was created.

To review:

- Since 1914, we've borrowed every dollar into existence.
- We pay interest on every dollar in existence.
- That interest is paid to a private bank, the Federal Reserve.
- The world's largest banks, not the government, own the Federal Reserve.
- The United States can't pay off its debt . . . it can only borrow more to pay the interest.
- Our government created income tax so we can pay this interest.

Welcome to the rabbit hole. Welcome to your new context.

Chapter 4

Greed, War, and the Dollar's Demise

With the outbreak of World War I, as with all the historical examples we've already covered in this book, the combatants halted redemption in gold, increased taxes, borrowed heavily, and created additional currency. However, because the United States did not enter the war for almost three years, it became the major supplier to the world during that time. Gold flowed into the U.S. at an astounding rate, increasing its gold stocks by more than 60 percent. When the European Allies could no longer pay in gold, the U.S. extended them credit. Once the U.S. entered the war, however, it too spent at a rate far in excess of its income. The U.S. national debt went from $1 billion in 1916 to $25 billion by war's end.

The world currency supply was exploding.

After the war, the world longed for the robust trade and economic stability of the international gold standard that had worked so well before the war. Thus, throughout the 1920s most of the world governments returned to a form of the gold standard. But the standard employed wasn't the classical gold standard of the prewar period. Instead, it was a pseudo–gold standard called the gold exchange standard.

Governments never seem to learn that you can't cheat gold. During the war, many countries inflated their currency supplies drastically. Yet when they tried to return to gold, they didn't want to devalue their currency against that gold by making the number of units of currency (gold certificates, or claim checks on gold) match the number of units of gold that backed that currency. So here's their "solution":

Building Pyramids

After the war, the United States had most of the world's gold. Conversely, many European countries had large supplies of U.S. dollars (and depleted gold reserves) because of the many war loans the U.S. had made to the Allies. Thus was decided that under the gold exchange standard, the dollar and the British pound, along with gold, would be used as currency reserves by the world's central banks and that the U.S. dollar and the pound would be redeemable in gold.

In the meantime, the U.S. had created a central bank (the Federal Reserve) and given it the power to create currency out of thin air. How can you create currency out of thin air and still back it with gold, you ask? You impose a reserve requirement on the central bank (the Federal Reserve), limiting the amount of currency it creates to a certain multiple of the units of gold it has in the vaults. In the Federal Reserve Act of 1913, it specified that the Fed was to keep a 40 percent reserve of "lawful money" (gold, or currency that could be redeemed for gold) at the U.S. Treasury.

Fractional reserve banking is like an inverted pyramid. Under a 10 percent reserve, one dollar at the bottom can be expanded, by layer upon layer of book entries, until it becomes $10 at the top. Adding a fractional reserve central bank, underneath fractional reserve commercial banks, was akin to placing an inverted pyramid on top of an inverted pyramid.

Before the Federal Reserve, commercial banks, under a 10 percent reserve ratio, could hold a $20 gold piece in reserve and create another $180 of loans, for a total of $200. But with the Federal Reserve as the foundation under the banking pyramid and having a reserve requirement of 40 percent, the Fed could put $50 in circulation for each $20 gold coin it had in the vaults. Then the banks, as the second layer in the pyramid, could create loans of $450 for a total of $500.

With the new gold exchange standard, foreign central banks could use dollars instead of gold. This meant that if the Federal Reserve had a $20 gold piece in the vault, and issued $50, then a foreign central bank could hold that $50 in reserve and, at a reserve ratio of 40 percent, issue the equivalent of $125 of their currency. Then when that $125 hit the banks, the banks could expand that to $1,250 worth of claim checks, all backed by a single, solitary $20 gold piece. That means that the real reserve ratio (the ratio of real money that could be paid out against their currency) was now only 1.6 percent.

Now there was an inverted pyramid, on top of an inverted pyramid, on top of an inverted pyramid. This was highly unstable. Ultimately, the gold exchange standard was a faulty system that governments imposed on their citizens, which allowed the governments to act as if their currencies were as valuable as before the war. This was a system that was destined for failure.

The Rise of Credit Culture

But every pyramid scheme flourishes in its early days, and so did the gold exchange standard. With all the new currency available from the central banks, the commercial banks generated many new loans. This abundance of currency led to the greatest consumer credit expansion thus far in American history, which, in turn, led to the biggest economic boom America had ever experienced. In a very real sense, credit put the roar in the Roaring Twenties.

Before 1913 the vast majority of loans had been commercial. Loans on nonfarmland real estate and consumer installment credit, like auto loans, were almost nonexistent, and interest rates were very high. But with the advent of the Fed, credit for cars, homes, and stocks was now cheap and easy. The effect of low interest rates combined with these new types of loans was immediate; bubbles sprang up everywhere. There was the Florida real estate bubble of 1925, and then of course the infamous stock market bubble of the late 1920s.

During the 1920s, many Americans stopped saving and started investing, treating their brokerage account as a savings account, much like many

Americans treated their homes in our most recent housing bubble. But a brokerage account is not a savings account, nor is a house. The value of a savings account depends on how many dollars you put in. But the value of a brokerage account or a house depends solely on the perception of others. If someone thinks your assets have value, then they do, but if they don't think they have value, then they don't.

In a credit-based economy, whether the economy does well or does poorly is largely based on people's perception. If people believe things are great, then people borrow and spend currency, and the economy flourishes. But if people have the least bit of anxiety, if they have doubts about tomorrow, then watch out!

In 1929, the stock market crashed, the credit bubble burst, and the U.S. economy slid into depression.

The Mechanics of a Depression

The popping of a credit bubble is a deflationary event, and in the case of the Great Depression it was massively deflationary. To understand how a deflation occurs, you need to know how our currency is born, and how it can join the ranks of the dearly departed.

When we take out a loan from a bank, the bank does not actually loan us any of the currency that was on deposit at the bank. Instead, the second the pen hits the paper on that mortgage, loan document, or credit card receipt that we are signing, the bank is allowed to create those dollars as a book entry. In other words, *we* create the currency. The bank is not allowed to do it without our signature. We create the currency, and then the bank gets to charge us interest for the currency we created. This brand-new currency we just created then becomes part of the currency supply. Much of our currency supply is created in this way.

But when a home goes into foreclosure, a loan gets defaulted on, or someone files bankruptcy, that currency simply disappears back into currency heaven where it came from. So as credit goes bad, the currency supply contracts, and deflation sets in.

This is what happened in 1930–1933, and it was disastrous. As a wave of foreclosures and bankruptcies swept the nation, one-third of the currency supply of the United States evaporated into thin air. Over the next three years, wages and prices fell by one third.

Run, Baby, Run

Bank runs are also enormously deflationary events because when you deposit one dollar into the bank, the bank carries that dollar as a liability on its books. It someday owes that dollar back to you. However, under a fractional reserve system, the bank is then allowed to create currency in the form of credit (loans), in an amount many times that of the original deposit, which it carries on its books as assets. As we've discussed, under a 10 percent reserve, a one dollar liability can create another $9 of assets for the bank.

This is normally not a problem, as long as the bank isn't loaned-up to the maximum amount permitted. With just a small amount of "excess" reserves, the bank can cover the day-to-day fluctuations because most of the time deposits and withdrawals come close to balancing out. But a serious problem can develop when too many people show up to make withdrawals at the same time without the counterbalancing effect of the relatively same amount of people making deposits. If withdrawals exceed deposits, the bank will draw from those "excess" reserves. Once those "excess" reserves have been used up, however, fractional reserve banking is then thrown into vicious reverse. From that point on, to be able to pay out one dollar against deposits, the bank must liquidate $9 of loans. This was what was happening in 1931, and it was one of the major contributing factors to the collapse of the U.S. currency supply.

Also, prior to the advent of the Federal Reserve, the public had about one dollar in the bank for each dollar in its pockets, and the banks kept one dollar of reserves on hand to pay out against each $3 of deposits. But thanks to the Federal Reserve, by 1929 the public had $11 in bank deposits for each dollar in its pocket, and the banks only had one dollar on hand to pay out against every $13 in deposits. This was a very dangerous situation. The public had lots of deposits and very little cash, and the banks also had very little cash to back up those deposits.

By November of 1930, bank failures were more than double the highest monthly level ever recorded. Over 250 banks with more than $180 million in deposits would fail that month. But this was only the beginning.

The largest single bank failure in U.S. history happened on December 11, 1930. The sixty-two-branch Bank of the United States collapsed. This failure would have a cascading effect, causing over 352 banks with more than $370 million in deposits to fail in that month alone. Worst of all, this was before deposit insurance. People's entire life savings were lost in the blink of an eye.

Then, to top it all off, on September 21, 1931, Great Britain defaulted from the gold exchange standard, throwing the world into monetary chaos. Foreign governments, along with businesses and private investors from the United States and around the world, began to fear that the U.S. might follow suit. Suddenly, there was a dash for cash.

Within the U.S., banks were running out of gold coin, and at the same time tremendous outflows of gold began to leave the vaults of the Federal Reserve, destined for far-off lands. The pyramid scheme that was the gold exchange standard began to crumble. To stop the bleeding, the Fed more than doubled the cost of currency in the U.S., raising the rates from 1.5 to 3.5 percent in one week.

As a result, between August 1931 and January 1932, 1,860 banks with $1.4 million in deposits suspended their operations.

However, 1932 was an election year. Three long years into the Depression people were desperate for a change, and in November, Franklin Delano Roosevelt was elected president. Even though his inauguration wouldn't be until March, rumors started flying that he would devalue the dollar. Again gold flowed out of the vaults as foreign governments, foreign investors, and the American public lost even more faith in the dollar, and the most devastating bank run in American history began. But this time the American public wouldn't be fooled.

As *Barron's* put it in its March 27, 1933, issue: "It has been aptly observed that the stages of deflation since 1929 have been the flight from property (chiefly securities) into bank deposits, next a flight from bank deposits into currency, and finally, a flight from currency into gold."

Incredibly, the currency supply of the United States was falling so fast that if it continued at that pace for a year only 22 percent of it would remain. The U.S. economic outlook was dire, and it seemed as if the dollar would fall into oblivion.

Executive Order

On March 4, 1933, Roosevelt was inaugurated, and within days he signed executive proclamations closing all banks for a "bank holiday," freezing foreign exchange, and preventing banks from paying out gold coin when they reopened. A month later he signed an executive order requiring U.S. citizens to turn over their private property (gold) to the Federal Reserve, in exchange for Federal Reserve notes.

On April 20, he signed another executive order, ending the right of U.S. citizens to buy, or trade in, foreign currencies, and/or transfer currency to accounts outside the United States. On the same day, the Thomas Amendment was sent to Congress, authorizing the president, at his discretion, to reduce the gold content of the dollar to as low as 50 percent of its former weight in gold. It was enacted into law on May 12, and then amended to give Federal Reserve notes the full "lawful money" status.

But there was still one major hurdle to overcome before Roosevelt could devalue the dollar: the infamous gold clause.

During the Civil War, President Abraham Lincoln had to come up with a way to pay the troops and introduced a second purely fiat currency to the country, the greenback dollar. When it first appeared, the greenback was worth the same amount as gold notes. But by the end of the Civil War they had fallen to just one third of the value of the gold-backed dollar. Many people who had made contracts or taken out loans before the war in gold notes paid them back in depreciated greenback dollars. Of course this was cheating the creditors and many lawsuits were filed.

After the end of the Civil War most contracts contained a "gold clause" to protect lenders and others from currency devaluation. The gold clause required payment in either gold or an amount of currency equal to the "weight of gold" value when the contract was entered into. The big problem for Roosevelt was that most government contracts and obligations also had this clause written into them. So devaluing the dollar would also increase the cost of government obligations by the same amount.

So at the behest of President Roosevelt, Congress passed a joint resolution on June 5 defaulting on the gold clause in all contracts, public and private, past, present, and future. In essence, the government simply said to American citizens and businesses, "We don't have to pay you." Outraged by what he viewed as the government's blatant disregard for Americans' rights, Senator Carter Glass, chairman of the Senate Finance Committee, lamented, "It's dishonor, sir. This great government, strong in gold, is breaking its promises to pay gold to widows and orphans to whom it has sold government bonds with a pledge to pay gold coin of the present standard of value. It's dishonor, sir." But Senator Thomas Gore of Oklahoma put it even more succinctly when he said, "Why, that's just plain stealing, isn't it, Mr. President?"

But these protests fell on deaf ears. On August 28, 1933, Roosevelt signed Executive Order 6260, outlawing the constitutional right of U.S. citizens to own gold. To keep from having to default on its commitments (declare bankruptcy), and to keep concealed the fraud of fractional reserve banking, the banking system's only choice was to get the government to make gold (the legal money of our constitution, an inert, inanimate element) illegal for U.S. citizens to own. Roosevelt gladly obliged.

First under threat of publishing the "gold hoarders'" names in the newspaper, and then under threat of fines and imprisonment, the United States of America, land of the *free* and home of the brave, ordered its citizens to turn over their own private property (the money in their pockets) to any Federal Reserve Bank. As far as I can tell, no one seems to know exactly who penned these proclamations and executive orders. But one thing was now clear. The government was no longer a government of the people, by the people, and for the people. Instead it was a government of the bankers, by the bankers, and for the bankers.

But there was still one more dastardly deed to be done.

Weight Watchers

On January 31, 1934, Roosevelt signed an executive proclamation effectively devaluing the dollar. Before this proclamation it took $20.67 to buy one troy ounce of gold. But now, since the dollar instantly had 40.09 percent less purchasing power, it took $35 to buy the same amount of gold. This also meant that, with regards to international trade, the government had just stolen 40.09 percent of the purchasing power of the entire currency supply of the people of the United States—all with the stroke of a pen. That is the power of fiat currency.

The worst part of this whole situation is that people who followed the rules and turned in their gold as decreed were the ones who suffered the most because those who illegally hung on to their gold realized a 69.33 percent profit due to the pressures Roosevelt's policies applied on the dollar. Less than 22 percent of the gold in circulation was turned in, however, and it seems not a single person was arrested or prosecuted for hoarding.

But despite the efforts of the U.S. government, gold won in the end. Gold and the will of the public forced the government's hand. By forbidding the U.S. population from laying claim to any of its own gold, and by devaluing the U.S. dollars, the United States was able to avert international runs on the dollar and was able to continue international trade under the gold standard. By declaring the claim checks on gold held by U.S. citizens null and void, and by requiring more claim checks from foreign central banks to purchase each unit of gold, there was now a far lower multiple of claim checks to gold, and the fractional reserve system was once again manageable.

Chart 2 shows the accounting that gold did of the U.S. dollar as a result. The gray line is U.S. base currency (dollars in circulation plus the paper dollars held

Chart 2. U.S. Monetary Base vs. Gold Reserves, 1918–1935

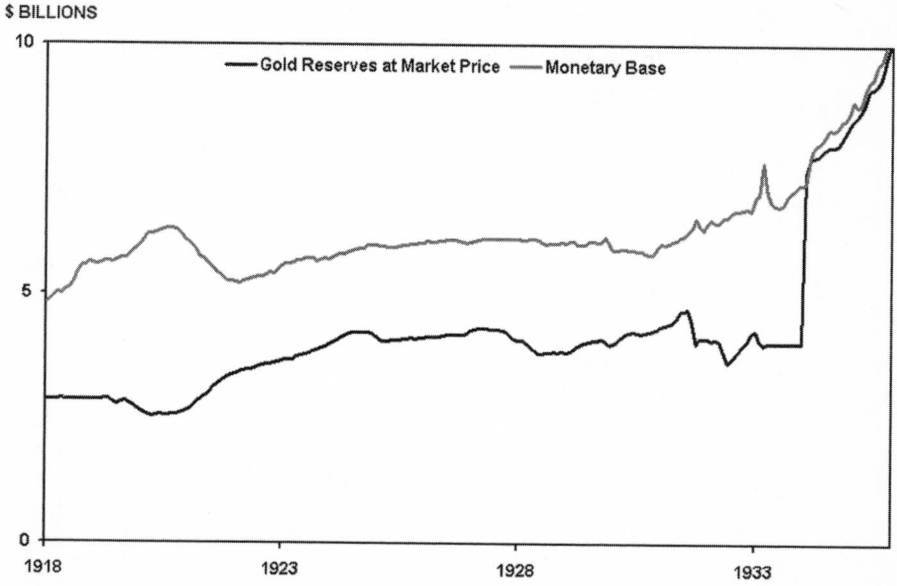

Source: St. Louis Federal Reserve Bank

at the Fed and in the banking system that are used as the base for fractional reserve credit dollars). The black line is the total value of the U.S. gold stock (the number of ounces the Treasury held times the price per ounce). By devaluing the dollar from one twentieth of an ounce of gold to one thirty-fifth of an ounce, the value of the gold held by the U.S. Treasury now exactly matched the value of the monetary base. This meant the dollar was once again fully backed by gold. It also meant that there was no reason for gold to continue being illegal since there was now enough gold to pay out against every paper dollar in existence, and the dollar could have been fully convertible into gold once again.

Gold had once again revalued itself, not with the knockout blow and the death of the currency as in previous chapters, but this time by a technical knockout. To halt the implosion of the U.S. banking system and to regain the trust of our international trading partners, gold had forced the government to devalue the currency by stealing from its citizens, and it had once again accounted for all the excess currency the banking system had created. Gold was still the undefeated heavyweight champion of the world.

But all the pain and suffering could have been avoided. Gold and silver require discipline and constraint from banks and governments, and both banks and governments resent gold for it. Numerous factors contributed to the Great Depression, but there was only one root cause. Governments around the world, along with the Federal Reserve, foreign central banks, and commercial banks, all tried to cheat gold.

Chapter 5

From Deep in the Woods the Golden Bull Came Charging

Bretton Woods

What got us out of the Great Depression wasn't the government spending and work programs of the Roosevelt administration, or even World War II, as most people think. No. What got us out of the Great Depression was the tremendous influx of gold from Europe. When the United States raised the price of gold by nearly 70 percent to $35 per ounce, prices of goods and services in the United States didn't immediately jump by the same 70 percent. Remember, thanks to the Roosevelt administration, the dollar was devalued by over 40 percent. So its purchasing power overseas fell by the same amount, slowing our imports dramatically. But countries buying from the U.S. now found their currency purchased 70 percent more U.S. stuff than it used to.

Also, when a country fixes its currency to gold, it has to buy or sell as much gold as is offered or demanded to maintain that currency price. Suddenly, all of the gold mining companies around the world were selling their gold to one buyer, the U.S. government. So this, plus a tremendous trade surplus, accounted for most of the gold inflows from 1934 through 1937.

But in 1938, a new dimension was added. When Germany's Adolf Hitler annexed Austria, the rest of Europe panicked, fearing the looming threat of war. And there was a transfer of wealth from European investments to U.S. investments as Europe braced for the ravages of war. European consumer goods factories were used to produce guns, ammunition, airplanes, and tanks. Thus most Europeans had to obtain everyday items from the U.S. So, in reality, gold inflows, foreign investment, and war profiteering, not social programs, were what lifted the U.S. out of the Depression.

At this point, the United States held approximately two thirds of the world monetary gold reserves and had a thriving economy. The U.S. produced more than half of the world's coal and two thirds of the world's electricity. Structurally, the U.S. was untouched by World War II, while its manufacturing base had grown fat selling armaments to Europe so that they could destroy each other's factories, and Europe had paid for those armaments with most of their gold. Very quickly world leaders realized the dire economic situation they were in. This huge trade imbalance meant that at the end of the war the world monetary system would be in shambles.

About a year before the end of the war, representatives from forty-four countries met in July of 1944 at Bretton Woods, New Hampshire, to figure out how they were going to make the world of international trade and finance work again. They needed a system of international payments that permitted trade without the wild fluctuations in currency exchange rates or the fear of sudden currency depreciation that had crippled international trade during the Great Depression.

It was decided that all countries would peg their currencies to the U.S. dollar and the U.S. would make the dollar redeemable in gold, to foreign central banks only, at a rate of $35 per ounce. This meant that, from World War II on, all foreign central banks *had* to hold dollars instead of, or in addition to, what was left of their gold reserves.

But there were two big flaws in the Bretton Woods system. Actually the flaws were more like big gaping holes.

First, there was no reserve ratio set as to how many dollars could be created for each unit of gold, allowing the U.S. to run trade and budget deficits and print the dollars to cover these deficits.

Second, even though U.S. citizens couldn't own gold, there was still an open gold market in the rest of the world, operating in parallel with the Bretton Woods gold market.

The Deficit War

The Vietnam War was the first large war where the American public wasn't asked to make financial sacrifices outside of paying taxes. We weren't asked to buy war bonds. We weren't asked to turn our consumer economy into a war economy. In fact, President Lyndon Johnson refused to pay for the war through taxation, and because the Bretton Woods system didn't require a reserve ratio, he was able to fund the entire Vietnam War through deficit spending. This truly was a deficit war. And on top of that, he added his Great Society programs, enacting a guns and butter policy that borrowed heavily to fund wars abroad and social programs at home.

But while we were waging a deficit-funded war in Vietnam, Charles de Gaulle, the president of France, was using the loopholes in the Bretton Woods system to quietly launch a full-blown assault on the U.S. dollar.

De Gaulle vs. the Dollar
Time magazine, Friday, February 12, 1965

Perhaps never before had a chief of state launched such an open assault on the monetary power of a friendly nation. Nor had anyone of such stature made so sweeping a criticism of the international monetary system since its founding in 1944 . . . [as] Charles de Gaulle last week [calling] for an eventual return to the gold standard. . . . Just before de Gaulle spoke, Treasury Secretary Douglas Dillon made the first public admission that the U.S. payments deficit in 1964 moved higher than anyone had expected. It totaled about $3 billion, all of which the U.S. is legally committed to exchange for U.S. gold on demand. The Federal Reserve announced that the U.S. gold supply declined last week by $100 million, to a 26-year low of $15.1 billion. [Note that the

deficit for 1964 is equal to 20 percent of the U.S. gold stocks.] . . .
France converted $150 million into gold last month, and plans another
$150 million conversion soon.

France withdrew from the London Gold Pool, a regulatory scheme that
was doomed to failure, whereby central banks would sell tons of gold into the
markets to keep the price of gold at $35 U.S., and resumed their redemption
of dollars for gold. Then Great Britain devalued the pound in November 1967,
causing a run on gold.

The pool was stretched to the breaking point, and the outflow of gold increased twenty-fold. By the end of the year more than 1,000 tons of gold had
left the vaults. For years Gold Pool sales had averaged five tons per day. By
March of 1968 sales were heading past 200 tons per day!

Take a look at Chart 3. It's the same as Chart 2, but with another twenty-
one years added. You can clearly see the rampant currency creation through
the mid- and late 1960s. You can also see that from 1959 to 1971, more than

Chart 3. U.S. Monetary Base vs. Gold Reserves, 1918–1971

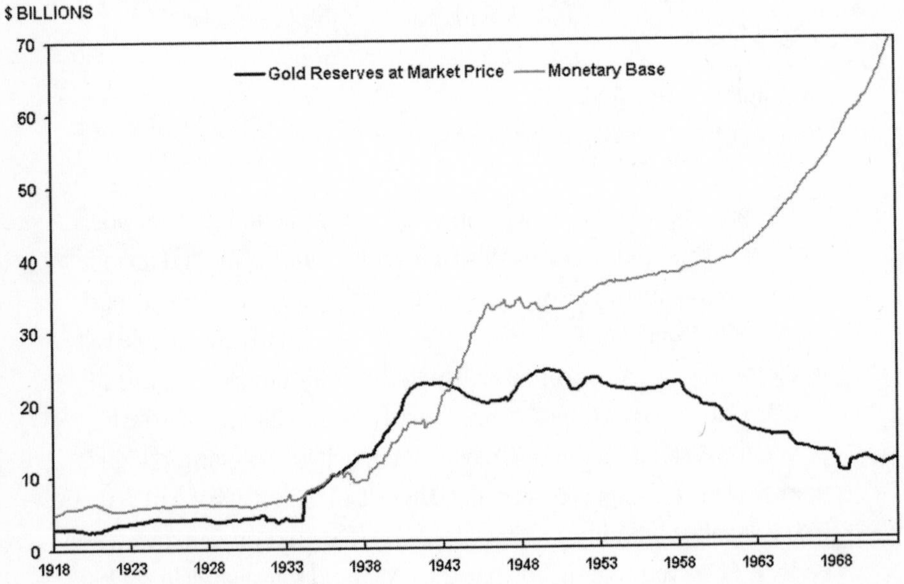

Source: St. Louis Federal Reserve Bank

50 percent of the U.S. gold left the vaults of the Treasury destined for far-off lands.

The Gold Pool was closed and the parallel free market for gold was allowed to find its own price. All the while, the official central bank price stayed at $35. Gold had the dollar on the ropes and delivered a one-two punch! Gold had won this round, but the fight was not over yet.

The Collapse of the Bretton Woods System

By 1971 the Bretton Woods system had been completely overwhelmed by the will of the public and the free markets. Gold had once again forced the government's hand, and on August 15, 1971, President Richard Nixon was forced to close the gold window. The U.S. dollar was no longer convertible to gold, and all currencies became free-floating. For the first time in U.S. history, the currency supply was entirely fiat. And since the Bretton Woods system had pegged all the world's currencies to gold through the dollar, all currencies on the planet became fiat currencies simultaneously. This was tantamount to the United States declaring bankruptcy. Gold had won this match, and it was now free to set its own value on the open market.

At this point most countries and central banks were now on a dollar standard, and were using dollars for international trade instead of gold. So with the end of the Bretton Woods system, in 1971, the dollar was freed from any fiscal constraints, allowing the U.S. to print as much paper "gold" as it wanted. A power it still holds today.

No other country has this hidden advantage, and now U.S. politicians seem to consider it their birthright. This advantage gives the U.S. the ability to run budget, trade, and other deficits and imbalances far in excess of anything the world has ever seen.

It also gives the U.S. the ability to tax not only its own population, but also the population of the entire world through the inflation caused by its deficit spending. Inflation of a currency supply respects no borders. Therefore, every new dollar that is printed devalues all other dollars everywhere in the world.

Yes, the dollar was free from the fiscal constraints of gold, but gold was also freed from the dollar. On August 15, 1971, gold became its own free-floating international money, no longer bound to any country.

The Golden Bull

After the collapse of the Bretton Woods system, all the debt that was created in the 1960s (monetary inflation) to fund the Vietnam War and the
Great Society came back with a vengeance in the form of price inflation in
the 1970s. Coincidentally, on August 15, 1971, the same day Nixon took the
U.S. off the gold standard, he reversed his position as a staunch believer in
the free market system and instituted wage and price controls, freezing
prices and wages for ninety days. History was once again repeating itself;
Diocletian had committed the same folly centuries before as the Roman
economy collapsed. But as unemployment soared, Nixon's intended ninety
days turned into a thousand days.

I remember seeing peach farmers protesting on the evening news by
dumping their peaches on the roadside and leaving them to rot because the
price they could legally sell them for was below their cost of production. I remember listening to Walter Cronkite's dry narration over images of dairy farmers pouring thousands of gallons of milk into empty fields, and chicken
farmers dumping thousands of live baby chicks into dumpsters until they were
full. Shortages ensued and store shelves were bare. Once again, it was proven
beyond a shadow of a doubt that government-managed markets do not work.
Nixon's effort was abandoned, and Secretary of the Treasury George Shultz
told the president, "At least we have now convinced everyone else of the right-
ness of our original position that wage-price controls are not the answer."

In October of 1973, the Yom Kippur War (also known as the Fourth Arab-
Israeli War) broke out. When much of the West supported the Israeli position,
the Organization of the Petroleum Exporting Countries (OPEC) cut production and placed an embargo on shipments to the United States as a punishment for its support of Israel. Most people think that this was a key factor
leading to the inflation of the 1970s. Again, they are mistaken.

Even though the Arab states were meting out punishment to the West for
supporting Israel, the bigger picture is that the purchasing power of the dollar had been falling since the United States started flooding the world with
dollars in the mid-1960s, and the price increases in oil only served to bring
the value OPEC received for a barrel of oil back up to the levels they had received under the Bretton Woods monetary system.

In 1973, the Shah of Iran, one of the U.S.'s closest allies in the region, told the *New York Times*, "Of course [the cost of] oil is going to rise. You increased the price of wheat you sell us by 300 percent, and the same for sugar and cement. . . . You buy our crude oil and sell it back to us, refined as petrochemicals, at a hundred times the price you've paid to us. . . . It's only fair that, from now on, you should pay more for oil. Let's say ten times more."

Although the price of oil measured in dollars increased dramatically, the price measured in gold had actually been falling. The rising dollar price of oil, back then, just as today, was only so that the producers of oil could recover the lost purchasing power of the dollar.

But it was still illegal for Americans to own gold. Then finally in 1971, a serious movement to restore Americans' right to once again own it emerged, led by a man named James Ulysses Blanchard III, who co-founded the National Committee to Legalize Gold. He held press conferences while brandishing illegal gold bars, publicly defying the federal authorities to throw him in jail. In 1973 he hired a biplane to tow a "Legalize Gold" banner over President Nixon's inauguration ceremony. He worked tirelessly lobbying Congress to get bills introduced, and his reward came on December 31, 1974, when President Gerald Ford signed the bill that made it legal for U.S. citizens to once again own gold.

Even though gold was now freely traded, it was not traded as a currency; instead it was traded as a commodity . . . at least at first. People had been using paper currency for so long that most had lost interest in gold and put their faith in paper.

Gold had started rising from $35 per ounce almost immediately after leaving the dollar. But in 1971, anyone who said it could reach $50 per ounce was considered crazy, and anyone who said that $100 was possible was tied up and hauled away. But by 1974 gold had reached almost $200 per ounce. Then in late 1978 it broke the $200 barrier and something changed in the character of how gold was traded and how the public viewed it. It was once again acting like a currency.

In June of 1979, *Time* magazine ran an article titled "Ingot we Trust," which said, "Quick-buck speculators, long-haul investors and just plain inflation-scared savers have put so much money into gold that last week it ballooned to a record $277.15 an ounce. . . . Predictions that gold could hit $300 an ounce by midsummer . . . are becoming self-fulfilling." People started lining up in front of coin shops, and the phones were ringing off the hook at the commodity exchanges. America had gold fever. But as gold moved past the $300 mark, the mainstream professionals and media started to warn that the top was near, and investors could suffer huge losses if they continued to buy gold.

But the mainstream was wrong. The gold fever was now turning into a twentieth-century gold rush. Just look at what *Time* magazine had to say in the article "Stampede for Precious Metal" from January 1980: "It was one of the most dazzling run-ups in history, and it underscored the enduring psychological lure of the yellow metal as the most consistently sought-after possession in times of strife and uncertainty. . . . In cities throughout the U.S. and Europe, people by the thousands lined up at jewelry and coin shops, lured by newspaper headlines of eye-popping new prices for gold and silver, and even by hourly news broadcasts on the radio."

I remember watching the local news broadcast at this time and seeing the helicopter shots of lines of people waiting to get into a local coin dealer. This dealer was located in the center of the block, on a major city street, and the line of people went out the front door, down the block, around the corner, and up the side street. The lines were being compared to those for *Star Wars* and *Apocalypse Now*!

I didn't buy gold back then. I was twenty-four years old and wrapped up in a business I had just started. But my father did, and so did the fathers of all of my friends. They were part of the masses of unsophisticated investors that were buying with the herd . . . and the herd always buys at the wrong time. From January 1975 through 1978 there were plenty of opportunities to buy gold between $100 and $200, but very few people did. It wasn't until gold broke $400 or more that the public caught on.

The strategy is simple: Buy low, and sell high. If you buy low, you don't need to try to time the exact top of a commodity upswing. Back in the 1970s, an investor who bought gold below $200 an ounce would have done amazingly well in just a couple of years and would have had plenty of time to sell at over $600. How many years does it take the Dow to triple? With gold, you could have done it in little more than one year. If you had bought at the bottom and sold at the top you would have realized eight and a half times your investment in less than three and a half years. And if you bought outside the U.S., in 1971, at the end of Bretton Woods, you would have made twenty-four times your investment.

Throughout history, governments and the banking system start with a certain amount of gold and silver. Then they make things "easier" on the population by storing the heavy gold and silver for us and printing receipts for us to use as currency. But the trouble is that they never stop printing. They produce more and more receipts until, one day, the public senses the debasement and suddenly, in an explosive move, gold's and silver's values catch up to all the receipts.

Chart 4 is, once again, the same as charts 2 and 3, but this time with a little twist. It runs longer, until 1985. And the black line is still the value of the U.S. reserves (number of ounces held by the Treasury, times the price of gold at the time), but the big difference is that, from the mid-1960s on, there are two gray lines. The lower gray line is the same U.S. base currency as in the last two charts, but the upper gray line is U.S. base currency plus revolving credit outstanding (unpaid credit card balances). I would argue that credit outstanding adds to the currency supply. Even though credit card dollars are phantom dollars, which sprang into existence with a signature, and are owed to the bank, they purchased a good or service when they sprang into existence. Once the seller of the good or service has that dollar it becomes a regular dollar that is not owed to a bank. It can therefore go on to purchase other goods and services and so becomes one of the drivers of price inflation. That phantom dollar circulates in the currency supply until someone earns it back and pays off their credit card debt with it. As long as credit outstanding is growing, so is the currency supply.

In this amazing chart you can see that gold once again did the accounting it has been doing for more than 2,400 years, since it did its first accounting in Athens, in 407 B.C. Even though the United States lost one half its gold from 1959 to 1971, the free markets and the will of the public caused gold's price to rise until it had done a full accounting. It rose until the value of the Treasury's stockpile surpassed the value of the monetary base at $135 billion. It continued to rise until it shot past the value of the monetary base plus revolving credit outstanding at $195 billion, and continued rising until it topped out at $225 billion.

Chart 4. Monetary Base & Revolving Credit vs. Gold Reserves 1918–1985

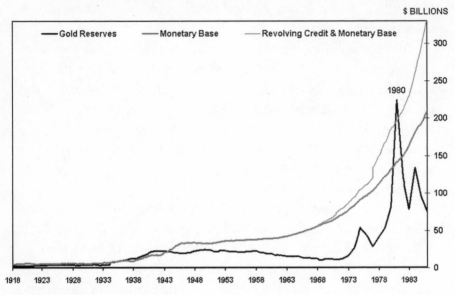

Source: St. Louis Federal Reserve Bank

Yes, gold did what it has always done. In a move that saw it rise more than twenty-four times (2,328.5 percent) from its Bretton Woods price of $35 per ounce, it revalued itself and accounted for all the paper dollars that had been printed since the last time it revalued itself, in January of 1934, and all the credit card debt. But the most amazing thing is that, once again, for a short while, the United States of America had the opportunity to go back on the gold standard.

But for investors it's a good thing that the Federal Reserve and the U.S. government chose not to go back on a gold standard. Because if they had, the greatest wealth transfer in the history of mankind would not be happening, and so the opportunity to have wealth transferred toward you would also not exist. But it is happening, and the wealth can be transferred toward you. Read on.

Chapter 6

Booms and Crashes

"Men, it has been well said, think in herds; it will be seen that they go mad in herds, while they only recover their senses slowly, and one by one."

CHARLES MACKAY, *EXTRAORDINARY POPULAR DELUSIONS AND THE MADNESS OF CROWDS*, 1841

The stock market crash of 1987 is known as Black Monday, but I call it Mysterious Monday because no one seems to know exactly why it happened. One thing is for certain; the crash of 1987 was the largest one-day crash in history. The most popular explanation was computer selling by program traders; others say it was a correction due to overvaluation, or blame it on lack of liquidity. One of the better explanations I've heard is that the preceding run-up was eerily similar to the run-up before the crash of 1929. Rumors spread, and the dynamics of herding and mass psychology took over.

The real cause of the crash probably goes back to the late 1970s and early 1980s. Paul Vocker took over as chairman of the Fed in August of 1979 and realized the need to raise real rates (interest rates minus inflation) into positive territory to get runaway inflation and the price of gold under control.

The higher rates only served to make a really bad recession worse, and by the time Ronald Reagan took over the White House in 1981 the economy was in bad shape. So, in March of 1983 the Fed goosed the economy by eliminating the reserve requirement on time deposits of thirty months or more, and in September changed it to eighteen months. In the two-year period from January of 1983 to January of 1985, the currency supply increased by a whopping 21 percent. On top of this vastly increased currency supply, the Fed reduced rates from over 11 percent in late 1984 to about 6.25 percent by late 1986.

All that currency had to go somewhere. The economy took off like a rocket, and the S&P 500 more than tripled, going from 100 points all the way up to 338. In a very short period of time, the index went from extremely undervalued to extremely overvalued in terms of earnings.

The investing public was caught up in a contagious euphoria similar to that of any other bubble and market crash in history. This euphoria made people believe, once again, that the market would always go up. However, due to extremely strong economic growth, inflation was becoming a concern. The Fed raised short-term interest rates to temper inflation. This had a negative effect on the markets.

On Wednesday, October 14, a sell-off began. By Friday the Dow had plunged more than 10 percent. Then on Monday, October 19, 1987, the majority of U.S. stockholders attempted to sell simultaneously. The market couldn't handle so many orders at once and most people couldn't sell because there weren't any buyers. The Dow lost 22.6 percent, and more than $500 billion of wealth was transferred in one day. The crisis wasn't just confined to the United States. Markets in Australia, Canada, Hong Kong, and the United Kingdom fell 41.8 percent, 22.5 percent, 45.8 percent, and 26.4 percent, respectively.

Fearing the crash might cause a worldwide depression, banking crisis, or both, the Fed intervened by increasing the currency supply, which had the side effect of taking the real estate booms that were happening in different pockets of the country and turning them into mini-bubbles.

The Real Estate Roller Coaster

During this time, home values skyrocketed. A close friend of mine owned a house in Los Angeles that she bought in 1970 for $64,000. In January of 1986 it was appraised at $425,000. By 1988, all that new currency that was created after the stock market bubble had popped just a year earlier was causing home prices to shoot up. At the end of 1989 my friend once again had her house appraised, but this time she was told it was worth $1.3 million . . . a whopping 200 percent increase in just four years! People in her area were trading homes like crazy. "For Sale" signs lined every block, and it seemed everyone was talking about real estate, buying real estate, or becoming a real estate broker.

All through 1988 and the first quarter of 1989 the Fed raised rates from just over 6.5 percent to almost 10 percent to try to stop the speculation frenzy. The Fed accomplished its objective, the property boom went bust, and a recession started on the East Coast, sweeping west across the country. Then on August 2, 1990, Iraq invaded Kuwait, and on January 17, 1991, the U.S. commenced operation Desert Storm. Once again we were in a war we couldn't afford, funded by deficit spending.

Home prices slid further and the country fell into recession. In response, the Fed cut the reserve requirement on time deposits from 3 to 0 percent, and in 1992 it cut the reserve requirement on transaction deposits from 12 percent to 10 percent. Over the same period, interest rates were slashed from 8 percent to less than 3 percent. But this time these measures had little immediate effect, and the economy continued to drag. Ironically, at the time of the writing of this book (nearly twenty years later) we again have a Bush as president (George W.), are in a war in the Middle East, housing prices are dropping dramatically, there is talk of interest rates being slashed to 2 percent (or less), and the economy is lagging.

Remember my friend with the $1.3 million house in 1989? Real estate prices in her neighborhood fell dramatically. One of her neighbors was a contractor who was building fourteen homes in the neighborhood. When homes stopped selling and prices started falling he was forced into bankruptcy, and all fourteen homes were foreclosed on. Banks don't want to own homes, they want to own mortgages on homes. So his bank put them all on the market at the same time, pricing them enough below the comparable properties in the neighborhood to insure their quick sale. Yet they still didn't sell. Then, within the next couple of months, two other banks had a wave of foreclosures that hit the market. Nothing was selling and everyone was trying to price their home just a little below the next guy to make sure their home was the next one that sold.

Real estate finally bottomed in my friend's neighborhood in the fall of 1992. Her neighbor, who lived directly across the street, sold his house at the end of 1992 for $425,000. Her house had a larger lot and a view, but still, it was worth less than half a million. The perceived value of her home had gone from $1.3 million to less than half a million in just three short years. Home prices in her neighborhood had plunged by 60 percent.

Right at the peak in 1989 one home on my friend's block sold for $1 million. Now, this home was almost considered a teardown. I saw it; it had peeling paint, a dead lawn, and had never been remodeled since it was built in the early 1950s. The new owner had put 20 percent down ($200,000) and still owed $800,000. Unfortunately for him, the prices for housing dropped dramatically and quickly. Eventually the value of that house bottomed out at $400,000. That meant he was upside down by $400,000, twice his initial equity.

To top it off, the Fed funds rate had plunged from nearly 10 percent when he bought the house in 1989, to just 3 percent by 1993, but the bank wouldn't refinance an $800,000 loan on a house that appraised at only $400,000. So, after putting $200,000 down, this poor guy was stuck with an $800,000 mortgage, at an interest rate of around 12 percent, and even though mortgage rates had fallen to 6 percent or less, he was unable to refinance. He was underwater for ten years until his home finally exceeded the 1989 purchase price in 1999.

Anyone who bought income property during the early 1990s, however, could easily get property that cash-flowed well, and soon after, real estate values appreciated more than anytime in the past.

All that fiddling the Fed did with reserve requirements and interest rates back in 1991 and 1992 finally kicked in with a vengeance in 1995. In 1995 the currency supply exploded and never looked back. In the decade from 1995 to 2005 the currency supply increased about 120 percent. That means that in those ten short years, more currency was created than in all the preceding eighty-three years. In fact, more currency was created than the entire previous history of the United States, and it resulted in the biggest real estate boom in history, as well as a whole bunch of bubbles in bonds, derivatives, consumption, debt, and once again, stocks.

Dot-Bomb

But the bubble of all bubbles—with maybe the exception of the recent real estate bubble—was the tech bubble of the late 1990s.

I'm not going to present a lot of facts, because I'm sure you remember the story.

It's a story that starts slowly with honest companies that came out with good products at the right time. Their quick rise and huge profits attracted other companies to jump on board the tech train. As that train accelerated, the masses lost their collective mind and threw money at companies of no substance. So basically, anyone with an idea could get together, incorporate, go public, buy Ferraris, install a golf course in their backyard with the proceeds, and issue stock like toilet paper.

Finally, in order to prevent a market meltdown from the Y2K bug, the Fed, with Alan Greenspan at the helm, pumped so much liquidity into the markets that they started to rise at an amazing pace.

The frenzied speculation sucked in so much capital that it eventually became a pyramid scheme, requiring an ever increasing mountain of currency to maintain its upward trajectory.

Essentially, the dot-coms turned into dot-bombs. The financial fallout included the popping of the dot-bubble, the collapse of companies such as Enron, WorldCom, and Global Crossing. Many investors lost their retirement funds, houses, and savings.

So, as you might have guessed by now, the lesson here is: If you jump into a market when everyone else is doing the same thing, you're probably too late. On the other hand, if you get into a market early, when it's fundamentally undervalued, then wait for it to become extremely overvalued, and sell once a true top has been established, you should do very well.

In the case of the Nasdaq, there were fourteen years where you could have bought your tech stocks while the index was under 1,000, and you had about a year to sell stocks over 3,500. If you timed it really well and were able to sell your tech stocks at 4,000 or 4,500, good for you. Unfortunately, that's when most people began buying, not selling. In the end, the bubble burst and lives were ruined.

It requires a lot of education and investigation to find an undervalued asset class at the beginning of a new bull market. Those opportunities only go to the very few who do the work required, and those that are able to think for themselves. Most investors get their advice from the same place as everyone else. They do things the easy way and wait for advice to come to them from the TV, the big investment firms, and their friends and neighbors who are already getting rich . . . on paper at least.

During the dot-com rush, most investors who bought into the mass media advice also bought into the pitch. They believed in the "new paradigm," and the sentiment that "tech will go up forever." They also bought their tech stocks *after* the Nasdaq passed 3,000 and held on, hoping for a turnaround as the index sank all the way past 2,000.

But remember, in times of financial upheaval, wealth is not destroyed, it is merely transferred. The opportunities this creates for the educated investor are enormous. The pain and suffering that was the popping of the Nasdaq bubble could have not only been avoided, but also capitalized on, by investors with the guts to change course when things didn't seem quite right (like when the Nasdaq went vertical in late 1999). I'm talking about investors that are educated enough to discern the difference between *price* and *value*. The price means nothing . . . value is everything.

Part 2

Today

Chapter 7

What's the Value?

Since the end of the Bretton Woods system in the 1970s, the dollar has been a dirty, double-dealing, back-stabbing liar, and it still is today.

As I write this chapter, the Dow is at 13,000 and is trying to push north toward its highs of just over 14,000. It also appears that we have just witnessed the end of the greatest real estate bubble of all time. The price of my friend's house in Los Angeles is on the decline again, and other home prices in her neighborhood have already fallen by 15 percent.

While you're reading this, the Dow could be blasting up past 15,000 or 20,000, and you're thinking, "14,000? Man, that was a long time ago." Or, it could be less than 10,000 and you're thinking, "14,000? Boy, those were the good old days." But it doesn't matter whether the Dow or real estate are up or down in price. Regardless of their price in terms of dollars, in terms of value, both the Dow and real estate have been crashing for years.

The Dow Is Crashing!

On October 4, 2006, the Dow broke its old high, set in the year 2000, of 11,750, and the financial press trumpeted, "Dow sets a new, all-time, record high!" However, the *value* of the Dow actually peaked in 1999–2001 and has been

crashing ever since. But if you have not yet educated yourself on the insidious ravages that inflation can have on your portfolio, you can't see it. This is
a blind spot investors must be mindful of, and guard against, if they are to
prosper.

Anytime that it looks like everything is going up, whether it be stocks,
bonds, real estate, commodities, and virtually every kind of investment you
can think of, you have to stop and ask yourself, "Why?" If stocks and real estate are soaring, shouldn't they be sucking currency away from other sectors?
The only reason the Dow looks like it is going up is because the Fed has
pumped so many more dollars into the currency supply that all asset classes
are rising . . . except the dollar! If everything is going up (getting more expensive), that means the dollar is going down.

Under these conditions, the only way to see where true value lies is to
eliminate the dollar from the equation. You have to measure each asset class,
not with the dollar, but against another asset class.

To get a picture of what's going on with stocks, I took the Dow as a representation of stocks (this is actually giving stocks an unfair advantage since
the Dow is the best performing index, but I'm going to fight this fight with
one hand tied behind my back) and then measured it against everything else
I could possibly think of. To do this I took the Dow and divided it into the
price of the other asset I am measuring it against.

Each chart will be the price of the Dow measured in "things" . . . like, how
many barrels of oil, or ounces of gold, does the Dow cost? The result? By measuring the Dow in terms of purchasing power it is clear that stocks have been
tanking for quite some time, even while their price has been rising relative to
the dollar. All of the following information is current as of April 2008.

Since January 2002, the dollar has plummeted negative 31.25 percent, versus other currencies. This has caused money (gold) to rise measured in currency (dollars) as more and more investors move out of their currency and
into real money.

In Chart 7, I measure the Dow the way you are used to seeing it, in dollars. But in Chart 8, I measure it with real money, not currency. It took almost
45 ounces of gold to buy one share of the Dow in 1999. As I write this it takes
less than 15. Here's another way of saying it: If you sold one share of the Dow

Chart 5. U.S. Dollar

Chart 6. Gold

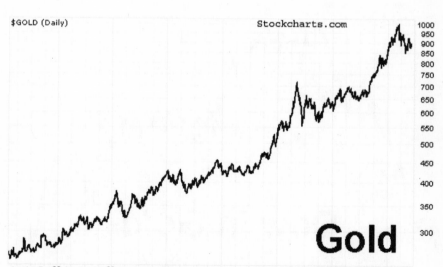

Chart 7. Dow in Dollars

Chart 8. Dow in Gold

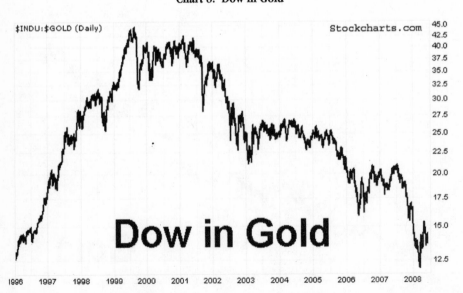

in 1999 you would have been able to buy 45 ounces of gold. At the writing of this book, the proceeds would only buy you 15. So measured in real money, the Dow has lost two thirds of its value, and crashed by 67 percent.

I like Charts 9 and 10, because they show you just how much real stuff (on the average) the Dow will buy you. They are the Dow divided by the Commodities Index and the Agricultural Price Index. Commodities are the stuff you buy, or the stuff that goes into the stuff you buy, while the Agricultural Index leans more toward the stuff you eat and wear. These charts include everything from copper and steel, to natural gas and heating oil, to livestock, grains, cotton, sugar, and orange juice. What these charts are saying is that you could buy three times as much stuff if you cashed out of the Dow in 1999 as the same number of shares will buy as I write this.

Here is probably the most important chart. Chart 11 shows you how many barrels of crude oil (our proxy for energy) you can buy with your proceeds from the Dow. If you sold one share of the Dow in early 1999 you could buy 800 barrels of oil. As I write this it only buys 100. Since 1999, the value of the Dow has plummeted 87.5 percent, measured against oil. But remember, oil

Chart 9. Dow in Commodities

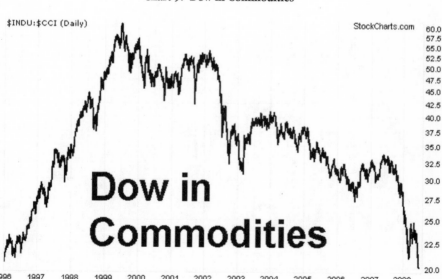

Chart 10. Dow in Food

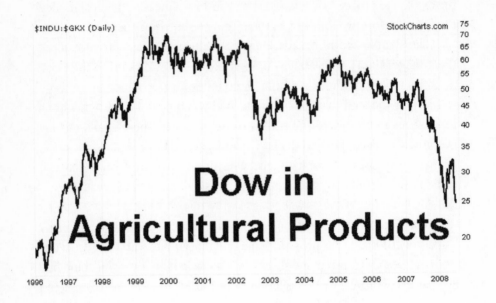

Chart 11. Dow in Crude Oil

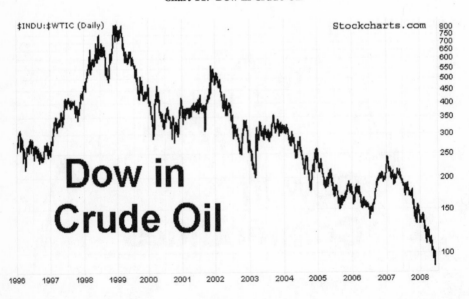

Chart 12. Dow in Industrial Metals

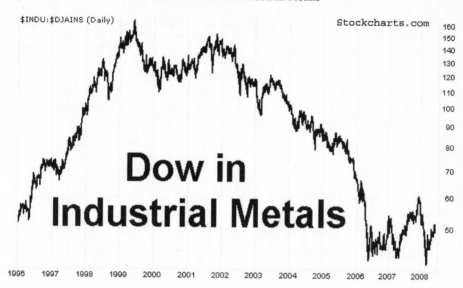

doesn't just end up as gasoline. It is the single most useful commodity there is. It's used to make medicines, fertilizers, plastics, tar for our roads, and the tires for your car.

Speaking of cars, along with plastics, cars are made of metals like steel, zinc, copper, and lead. Chart 12 shows that, measured against the Dow Jones Industrial Metals Spot Price Index, the Dow has crashed by 75 percent. And believe it or not, this is one of the reasons the U.S. car companies are doing so poorly. Just take a look at the stocks of GM and Ford over the same time frame. They've crashed by about the same percentage because the automakers' costs are up, and profits are gone.

In Chart 13, I show the relative performance of the Dow (bottom line), gold (middle line), and silver (top line). As a starting point, I selected the beginning of the precious metals bull market in 2001. All three start on the left-hand side of the chart grouped together on the zero line. The chart shows the relative performance in percentage gains. As you can see, measured from 2001, the Dow has risen only 15 percent, while gold shot up 250 percent, and silver rocketed 300 percent!

Chart 13. Relative performance of Dow, gold, and silver

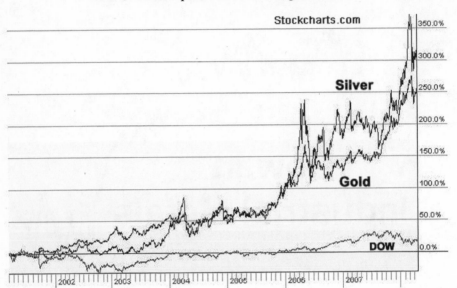

Call the Cops . . . We've Been Robbed!

Why is this happening? Why does everyone think the Dow and real estate are going up in value, when they are actually going down in value? The answer is inflation.

According to the Minneapolis Federal Reserve, total inflation from 2000 to 2008, using the Consumer Price Index, was just about 22 percent. But, unfortunately, the CPI is an unreliable measuring stick. Here's why.

In calculating inflation, the Bureau of Labor Statistics (BLS) takes a basket of goods and services and tracks their prices throughout the years. This worked just fine when they would track the actual price of the same items year after year. The problem is the BLS no longer uses the actual price, and they no longer track the same items year to year. For example, if the price of an item has changed dramatically from one year to the next (which as you might imagine might make whoever is in the White House look bad) the item can be dropped from the basket of goods (deletion), substituted with another item (substitution), or simply assigned a new price (hedonic adjustment).

For an example of deletion, you need look no further than the BLS and the mainstream media. A while back the BLS came out with a "new and improved" measure of inflation, called Core-CPI, which excludes the only two things that you absolutely need to survive, and would die without, food and energy. This is the inflation statistic that most of us hear because it's the most reported by the press. The argument is that food and energy prices are volatile and seasonal, and removing them makes a more consistent measure of inflation. According to the Energy Information Administration, for instance, the average price of gasoline at the turn of this century was $1.29. So, according to the government's total inflation figure of 22 percent from 2000 to 2008, gasoline should cost $1.57 in 2008.

As for substitution, I'll give you a quote directly from the BLS's Web site. Price inflation was raging during the Reagan administration, and this was when it first turned the CPI into what I call the CP-Lie. Homes were getting more expensive than they liked, so the BLS decided that we don't actually own our homes, we really rent from ourselves: "On February 25, 1983, the Bureau of Labor Statistics (BLS) introduced an important technical modification in the Consumer Price Index for All Urban Consumers (CPI-U). This altered the treatment of housing costs by shifting the costs for homeowners to a rental equivalent basis. The new treatment of housing costs was incorporated into the Consumer Price Index for Urban Wage Earners and Clerical Workers (CPI-W), used to index social security benefits, in 1985." This change makes inflation look lower whenever real estate prices go up faster then rents.

But don't think I'm criticizing just Republicans, because both parties love the CP-Lie . . . it makes them look good. The Democrats' way of doing things is to figure, "Well, if beef gets too expensive, people will eat chicken instead." And that's just what the BLS did under the administration of President Bill Clinton. It took out the cut of choice top sirloin beef that it had been tracking since 1959, and substituted chicken breast, because it was cheaper, which makes the CP-Lie lower.

When it comes to hedonic adjustment, nobody says it better that Adam Hamilton of zealllc.com, in his article "Lies, Damn Lies, and the CPI": "By using the mathematical equivalent of tea leaves and goat bones, the BLS statisticians have created a surreal new reality where the 'true quality adjusted' price of different goods may be 'computed.'" Hedonic adjustment is supposed to compensate for improvements in quality. In other words, if the car you bought this year cost you 5 percent more than the car you had last year, but the new car has stability control, then they figure the price increase was offset by the quality improvement, so the cars actually cost the same, according to the BLS.

One might ask, Why is the Bureau of *Labor* Statistics doing these calculations? Labor really has nothing to do with it. Rather, shouldn't the Bureau of Statistics calculate them? Indeed, it would be much more appropriate for these statistics to come from the Bureau of Statistics (or as I like to call it, BS).

So what would price inflation look like if they used the original CPI instead of the CP-Lie? John Williams of Shadow Government Statistics (Shadow-Stats.com), and Bart at Nowandfutures.com make it their job to haunt our government and expose its financial shenanigans. They have painstakingly reconstructed the pre-propaganda version of the CPI. One look in your wallet, and you'll know they're right.

Here's is one of John Williams's charts of the CPI with the smiley faces removed (Chart 14). The top black line is the re-created CPI, and the gray line at the bottom is the official CP-Lie.

Chart 14. CPI vs. ShadowStats.com Alternative

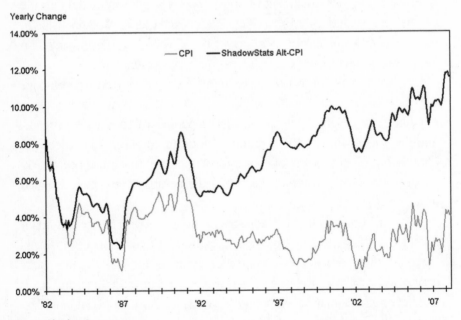

Source: ShadowStats.com

My definition of inflation is an expansion of the currency supply (which is incorrectly referred to as the *money* supply). Rising prices are not inflation, but the symptom of inflation. Every newly created unit of currency dilutes the pool of currency already in circulation, thereby reducing its value. This happens because the increased quantity of currency is still chasing after the same number of goods and services, thereby bidding up prices. The inherent value of a consumer good remains the same, it's the amount of currency required to purchase that good that rises.

The Federal Reserve has different ways of measuring the currency supply. The broadest one, meaning the one that counts the most dollars, is called M3, and they've reported M3 every month since January 1959. But on March 23, 2006, the Fed decided to hide M3 from us, and they stopped publishing the data. Why? Do you think it could be because they intend to significantly inflate the currency supply?

By the time this book hits the shelves, the M3 currency supply of the United States will be approximately $14 trillion. Now hold on to your hat because this one's going to hurt: Since 2000, the Fed has increased the M3 currency supply by a whopping 112 percent! Thus, any investment that has returned less than 112 percent over this time period is underwater. This means that the Dow would have to be above 25,000, not 14,000, to have the same value it had back at the turn of this century. And now it is estimated that M3 is inflating at a rate of about 18 percent per year and rising. I would expect that prices could follow suit within a couple of years.

Note that in Chart 15, the rate of currency creation today has already exceeded the rate of currency creation that kicked off the great precious metals bull market of the 1970s. This is only the very beginning of what I believe will turn out to be the greatest bull market in history.

The point of all this talk about currency supply is to open your eyes to the fact that the dollar is simply a smoke screen that obscures true value, and that allows the Fed to legally steal from your back pocket while patting you on the shoulder and telling you they'll make everything all right.

Now here's an amazing chart (Chart 16). It shows cumulative inflation in the United States from 1774 to 2007. Note that back when we used real money, inflation netted out to zero. As you can see, with the inception of the Federal Reserve the official inflation rate became significantly lower than the actual

Chart 15. M3 Growth with ShadowStats.com Continuation

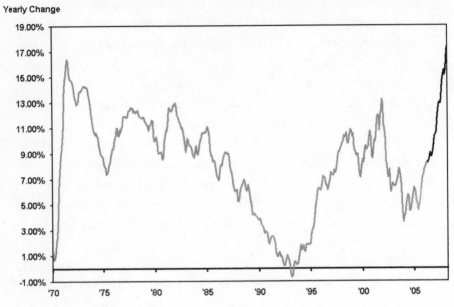

Source: ShadowStats.com

Chart 16. Inflation 1774–2007

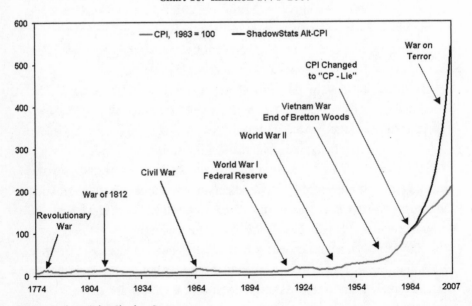

Source: Robert Sahr, ShadowStats.com

inflation rate. The point at which the two lines diverge is when they began fiddling with the CPI. The line on the bottom is the CP-Lie. The dark line on the top, which has the trajectory of a rocket to the moon, is the real CPI.

The Hidden Tax and the Invisible Crash

There are basically two kinds of tax, the kind the masses can see, and the kind they can't. The inflation tax is of the second kind. Whenever a politician promises you more free stuff than the guy he's running against, whenever the masses think they're getting something for nothing, whenever our government engages in deficit spending, whenever we borrow the prosperity of tomorrow to spend today, it comes back to haunt us in the form of an inflation tax, which insidiously, and invisibly confiscates our wealth. The greatest advantage an investor can have is to understand that fact and exploit it.

Just to drive the point home, here is a chart (Chart 17) of the Dow (black line) from the year 1914, when the Fed opened for business, showing the 1929 crash and the spectacular bull run from 1932 through today. "But wait a minute," you might ask, "what's that other line doing there?" That, my friend, is the Dow's value inflation-adjusted using the CP-Lie (dark gray line) and the re-created original CPI (light gray line).

Note that when you account for the stealth tax of inflation, in 1966 the Dow began a long, slow crash that would see it lose value over the next sixteen years. Chances are you never heard of the crash of 1966, but I assure you it happened, and it resulted in the raging price inflation of the 1970s eating away at investor profits. Economists refer to it as "The Invisible Crash" because investors never knew what hit them.

The Dow failed to sustainably surpass 1,000 points from 1966 to 1982. If you had put $100,000 in the Dow in 1966, by 1982 your $100,000 was still $100,000, but due to inflation it would only buy you $34,000 worth of goods and services as measured by the 1966 CPI. That represents a 66 percent loss in value. That is how the inflation tax can cause an invisible crash.

Many who invested in the Dow between 1966 and 1982 felt they were making a safe and prudent investment decision. They bought into the pundit hype that investments in stocks do well over long periods of time. All the while their currency was losing its value at an average rate of 6.52 percent per

Chart 17. Dow vs. Inflation Adjusted Dow

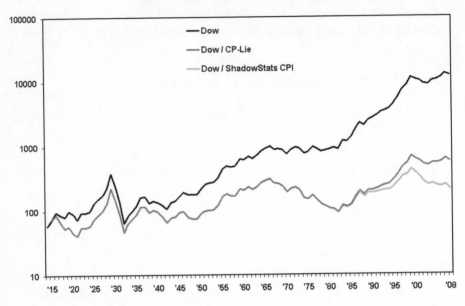

Source: Minneapolis Federal Reserve Bank

year (66 percent loss spread over sixteen years). As we will see later in the book, a smart investor would have recognized the ravaging effects inflation was having on their portfolio, and would have moved their money into investments that exploited the weakness of the U.S. currency. Any guess what those investments might be? I'll give you a hint. They're the topic of this book.

Beyond the shadow of a doubt the general equities markets (aka stock markets) are crashing, and have been since as early as 1999 and as late as 2001, depending on how you measure it. Even though the Dow is going up in *price*, its *value* is falling. If everything else is going up in price faster than the Dow, then it stands to reason that the Dow is crashing in relative terms. In fact, I can't think of any way you can measure the Dow that doesn't show it crashing . . . except of course, dollars. Just as there was an invisible crash from 1966 to 1982, there is an invisible crash happening now, as I write, and just as it was last time, the hidden tax of inflation is the cause.

An invisible crash is a product of a fiat currency system and/or rampant credit creation. It requires a rapidly expanding currency supply to obscure the fact that an overvalued asset class is correcting and reverting to fair value, or less. It cannot happen on a gold standard with conservative fractional reserve banking practices. Therefore, it didn't happen in the United States until Johnson started to cheat the Bretton Woods system to fund the Vietnam War, and it accelerated when Nixon ended Bretton Woods, taking the United States off the gold standard in 1971. But it has happened numerous times throughout world history when a country leaves an asset-backed currency for a fiat currency. We've already seen this in our examples of John Law's France and the German Weimar hyperinflation. Those are just two of many throughout history. The pattern is always the same. It never changes. Therefore, if you understand the pattern, you can use it to your advantage.

Value Versus Price

So this discussion begs the questions: Can an investor prosper under such conditions? Is there a way to beat inflation?

Absolutely! In fact, a smart investor can achieve superior results under these conditions. How? Because anytime you find yourself in a situation where you are the informed investor and the masses don't yet know what's going on, you have the advantage. Once the cycle has changed, and once you've verified that conditions have shifted, you can flourish. Any investor that does reasonable due diligence, takes a position early, waits for the masses to wake up, and hangs on for the ride, has an extremely good chance of making boatloads of money.

Question: So how do I see what the value of something truly is? How do I see past the lie of the dollar?

Answer: You must stop measuring value with the dollar. The dollar can't tell you what true value is because it *can't* tell the truth. To borrow a phrase coined by Al Franken, the dollar is a "lying liar."

People always ask me, "How high will gold go?" The answer they are expecting from me is a price in dollars. Stop thinking that way! It's not what the price of gold is that matters, but rather how much stuff it will buy. If I said, "Gold is going to a million dollars an ounce," most people would say, "Great!", and run out and buy as much gold as they could. But then if I said, "But a cup of coffee is going to cost a billion," then they'd say, "Let's see . . . that means coffee cost a thousand ounces of gold a cup. That's not so great." Under those conditions people would sell all their gold while it was still worth something, and not wait until it went up to a million dollars an ounce and effectively worth nothing.

Question: Why do I keep harping on "true value"?

Answer: Because it's the only way to tell whether an asset class is over-valued, or undervalued, and nothing is more important to an investor.

So how do you measure true value? As I've already mentioned, the first step is to stop relying on the dollar and start using things with inherent value to measure other things with inherent value.

By way of example, let me ask you this: What's the value of your house? You probably know the price, but what's the value?

Here's how to find out. Most people know what other homes are selling for in their neighborhood, so just make a guesstimate of the price of your house. Then divide the price of the house by the current points of the Dow and you'll know how many shares of the Dow your house is worth. Now take the price of your house and divide it by the price of gold and you'll know how many ounces of gold your house is worth. Then take the price of your house and divide it by the price of a barrel of crude oil and you'll know how many barrels of oil your house is worth.

This information might seem worthless, but once you analyze it in a historical framework, using something besides currency to measure your current value, you'll discover that, over time, almost nothing goes up. Seriously. Measured in currency, things appear to go up in value, but they're only going up in price. Measured in value, everything just zigzags sideways throughout time. If you graph it you'll see that almost everything in terms of value goes from undervalued to overvalued to undervalued and back again, over and over. Once you learn to recognize the patterns of value cycles, then information is worth everything.

You might be thinking to yourself, *What causes things to go from over-valued to undervalued?*

Value shifts when the public rushes from one asset class to another. The public generally chases whichever asset class is the hottest, is on the cover of *Time* and *Newsweek*, is on late night infomercials advertised as the best way to get rich, and is the one that everyone is jumping onto the bandwagon for.

Those are the asset classes that are sucking capital away from other asset classes. And by doing so, the one that's hot becomes overvalued. The one that's not becomes undervalued. It's really that simple.

From the end of World War II to 1966, the hot assets were stocks and real estate. From 1966 to 1980 it was commodities (and gold, once it was no longer our currency). From 1980 to 2000 it was stocks and real estate. And, at this turn of the century, the hot asset class became gold and commodities once again. Those who are truly financially intelligent are able to not only recognize these cycles, but use the information to capitalize on them as well.

Now that you have an understanding of true value and the history of how gold and silver revalue themselves throughout the centuries, let's take a look at the fuel that will propel gold's and silver's stellar performance for the foreseeable future.

Chapter 8

The Dark Cloud

"New houses were built in every direction, and an illusory prosperity shown over the land, and so dazzled the eyes of the whole nation, that none could see the dark cloud on the horizon announcing the storm that was too rapidly approaching."

CHARLES MACKAY, *EXTRAORDINARY POPULAR DELUSIONS AND THE MADNESS OF CROWDS*, 1841

In the beginning of this book we talked about the coming perfect economic storm. In this chapter we'll cover the dark clouds that are getting ready to converge into this storm. Believe it or not, I wish I could just skip this chapter. There are a many doomsday books out there, and I wanted to keep this book upbeat. But that would be irresponsible of me because it is the trends covered in this and the next chapters that will be the main drivers for the amazing future increase in the true value (purchasing power) of the precious metals.

I have to admit that when I first started researching this chapter it scared me, and I developed a bunker mentality. Then I met Robert Kiyosaki, and he changed my attitude in a matter of minutes, pointing out that bigger crises lead to bigger opportunities. I could hide in my bunker and emerge after the destruction to come, or I could profit from the impending storm. That is why I have so much respect for Robert and what he does. Rather than take his knowledge and wisdom, and profit for himself, he believes in educating everyone he can. His desire is to see lives changed for the better by his message of financial education and intelligence. And by golly, that is a message I can get on board with.

Yep, a Storm's A'Comin'

In old movies, you'll sometimes see the wise old farmer, dressed in overalls and a plaid shirt, maybe even chewing on some wheat, look out to the horizon and remark, "Looks like a storms a'comin." How does he know? Well, he's been living on and farming that land for many years, and he's learned to recognize the signs. If our idealized farmer were to look out at today's financial horizon, he'd definitely say a storm is coming. He might suggest that you move your livestock to a safer place, lock the barn doors, and secure the storm windows. This financial storm is going be dark and terrifying, but I promise, if you heed the warnings and move your resources into safer areas, specifically precious metals, it'll be bright and sunny for you once the storm has passed.

As I said, I really do wish I could skip this chapter, but it really is one of the most important chapters in the book because these coming problems are the launch pad for gold's and silver's rocket ship to the moon. These problems also add up to the potential death of the dollar. They may not be the final nail in the coffin but, they're definitely the boards and planks.

The problems I'm talking about are the global trade imbalances, budget deficits, and rampant currency creation, but most of all, the really big killer, the total U.S. debt and its unfunded liabilities.

Mountain of Debt

On March 16, 2007, Congress passed a bill to increase the ceiling on the national debt from $8.2 trillion to $9 trillion. But as I'm writing this, just a few months later, the debt is already $8.98 trillion, and Congress has just approved the fifth increase on the debt ceiling in the last six years, raising it to $9.8 trillion. This $850 billion increase should last another few months, and it's entirely possible that the national debt could surpass $10 trillion by the end of 2008. This means that a baby born as a U.S. citizen in 2007 comes into the world owing approximately $30,000. But that's only what the baby owes for our reckless deficit spending in the past (debt). What about all the reckless deficit spending promised to future generations like Social Security and Medicare?

Unfunded Liabilities

Programs like Social Security and Medicare are unfunded liabilities. They are promises made to our citizens that will have to be paid for someday in the future. Unfunded simply means that when our government made the promises, they didn't figure out (or in some cases even think about) how they would pay for them in the future.

Former U.S. Comptroller General David Walker says that U.S. unfunded liabilities grew from $20 trillion in 2000, to $50 trillion in 2006. In 2000 the U.S. gross domestic product (GDP), a measurement of the value of all the goods and services produced in the country in one year (a measurement of the size of the economy), was about $10 trillion, and in 2006 it was about $12.5 trillion. That means our unfunded liabilities were two times GDP in 2000, but four times GDP just six years later. So, the economy grew 25 percent over this period, but the unfunded liabilities grew by 150 percent. The unfunded liability monster is growing six times faster than the U.S. economy.

It now totals more than 95 percent of the entire household net worth of the United States and is expected to exceed household net worth within just a few short years.

Michael Hodges, a concerned father and grandfather, publishes the "Grandfather Economic Report." I encourage you to check out this report. It's fantastic. Hodges has gone even further in analyzing debt than just unfunded liabilities. Instead, he has taken all of the state and local government debt, household debt, business sector debt, plus financial sector debt, U.S. federal debt (referred to as the national debt), and added it to the unfunded liabilities. The total outstanding U.S. debt he presents is staggering.

How big is the problem according to Hodges? It is now a $160 trillion problem and growing at a daily rate that far exceeds the growth of the U.S.

economy. That's over a million dollars per family. It means every man, woman, and child in the United States owes $550,000 . . . even a newborn baby. "Welcome to the world kid. Here's the bill!"

$160 trillion is a mind-boggling figure, so to give you an idea of just how large it is: If you spent one dollar every second, twenty-four hours a day, 365 days a year, it would take you twenty-four times longer than the entire existence of modern man to spend 160 trillion dollars. If you took twenty-two one-dollar bills, laid them on the ground, side by side, and then kept stacking more dollar bills on top of them, by the time you stacked 100 trillion of them all sixteen stacks would reach the moon. And you'd still have enough change left over to bury Los Angeles. Who needs earthquakes when you've got the national debt?

Have our politicians in Washington gone crazy? Have we all gone insane? Are we spending ourselves into a hole that we'll never be able to climb out of? The answers are, yes, yes, and YES!

A Voice of Reason

For several years now David Walker, who not only was U.S. Comptroller general but also was head of the Government Accountability Office (GAO), effectively the chief auditor and accountant for the largest economy in the world, has been on an aggressive road tour, speaking to anyone who will listen about the dangers of the United States' reckless spending spree.

He believes U.S. fiscal policy is the greatest threat to our well-being as a nation. Here's what he had to say about it on *60 Minutes*: "I would argue that the most serious threat to the United States is not someone hiding in a cave in Afghanistan or Pakistan but our own fiscal irresponsibility."

In fact, Walker had become so disenchanted by the federal government's fiscal recklessness that he resigned on March 12, 2008.

Walker has this to say about America's unfunded liability monster:

The problem is that in the coming decades, there simply aren't going to be enough full-time workers to promote strong economic growth or to sustain existing entitlement programs. Like most industrialized nations, the United States will have fewer full-time workers paying taxes and contributing to federal social insurance programs. At the same time, growing numbers of retirees will be claiming their Social Security, Medicare, and Medicaid benefits.

Unless we reform Social Security, Medicare, and Medicaid, these programs will eventually crowd out all other federal spending. Otherwise, by 2040 our government could be doing little more than sending out Social Security checks and paying interest on our massive national debt.

The issues he's talking about are all covered in the consolidated financial statement of the United States. Anyone can go to the GAO's Web site and download a copy at www.gao.gov, or the Treasury's Web site, www.fms.treas.gov. I print out a copy every year and keep it on my desk for reference.

The following charts are taken directly from the report. Here's Medicare measured as a percentage of gross domestic product (Chart 18). The solid line

Chart 18. Medicare Part B and Part D Premium and State Transfer Income and Expenditures as a Percent of GDP 1970–2081

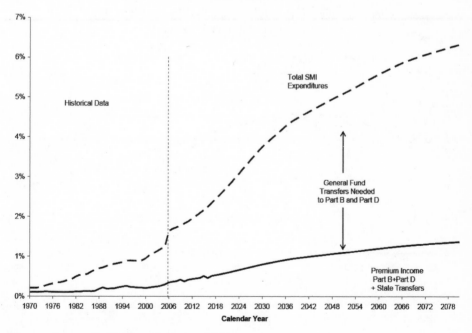

Source: Centers for Medicare & Medicaid Services

is how much income the government expects to take in to pay for it, and the broken line is how much the government expects it to cost.

That big jump in the expenses (broken line) is the 2006 "landmark" Medicare prescription drug bill that David Walker often talks about in his speeches.

The next graph (Chart 19) shows the projections for the George W. Bush administration's proposal for a balanced budget by 2012 (solid line), with David Walker's more realistic projections. It surprises me, however, that Walker would use this graph as a baseline because the baseline is based on fantasy numbers in the first place.

Notice that the graph starts in the year 2000 with a surplus. The notion that there was a surplus at the end of the Clinton years is another lie. There was no real surplus because the federal government uses a cash accounting that allows a little room for monetary magic. The last year Clinton was in office the national debt grew by $68.6 billion, so the "real" deficit was $68.6 billion. Clinton misled us, and I'm not talking about Monica Lewinsky or what the meaning of "is" is. There was actually a deficit in 2000, because the debt grew.

Chart 19. U.S. Unified Surpluses and Deficits as a Share of GDP Under Alternative Fiscal Policy Simulations

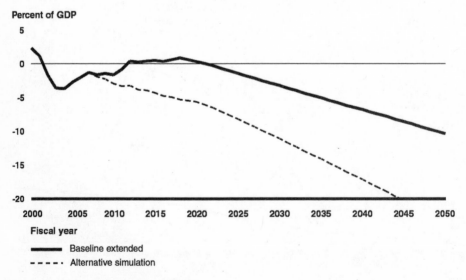

Source: St. Louis Federal Reserve Bank

But I'm not just going to beat up on Clinton. My political bashing is completely nonpartisan. So, we actually started with a budget that was nowhere near being balanced in 2000. That means that in the chart of the balanced budget projection, you have to imagine the projections lowered down so that it begins at the zero line. Then you can see Bush's tax cuts put us in the hole by about 9 percent, causing the deficit to explode again. By 2005 the reported deficit was $318.6 billion, yet the debt grew by $760.2 billion (real deficit), eleven times greater than when Bush took office. Then on top of that, Bush added the $8 trillion Medicare prescription drug benefits package. With one stroke of the pen, Congress and George W. Bush increased existing Medicare obligations nearly 40 percent.

Both parties provide bountiful amounts of idiotic fiscal policy. In fact, this accounting apparition began under Ronald Reagan (Chart 20).

In 1981, Reagan signed the Kemp-Roth tax cut, increasing the deficit by more than two and a half times in just two years, from $79 billion to $208 billion. Then in 1982, projections were made showing that the Social Security Trust Fund would be insolvent by the following year. (The odd thing was that

Chart 20. Social Security Trust Fund Assets

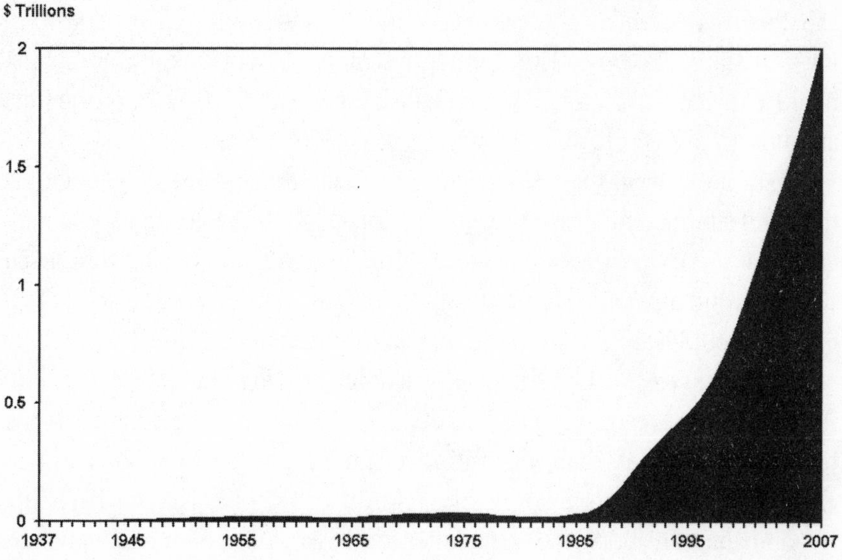

$ Trillions

Source: Social Security Administration

1982 saw a $598 million surplus in Social Security.) So a commission was appointed to study the insolvency problem, and in 1983 Ronald Reagan signed an amendment to "save" Social Security. Then in 1984, Social Security expenditures crept up at their normal pace, while revenues started to skyrocket.

Now that the Social Security Trust Fund had "excess" assets, the U.S. Treasury began borrowing the assets and replacing them with bonds (IOUs). The borrowed assets were then added to the general fund and spent. Basically, they took from one cookie jar to stock another.

Within a few years there was an extra $20 billion to $30 billion per year for the government to pillage. So the federal masters of illusion cut our income tax, increased our Social Security tax, and then stole the assets to help make up for the deficit caused by the tax cut. And they call this a *trust* fund? But don't worry; the government says this debt doesn't count because we owe it to ourselves. In fact, they're pretty sure this debt will support us all in our retirement. Good luck!

Oh yeah, this was also the act that made Social Security benefits (which are nothing more than a tax that you have paid being returned to you) taxable. That, my friend, is called double taxation, and it was signed into effect by a conservative icon.

But Social Security isn't the only federal agency that's been pillaged. In the U.S. financial statement there is a page titled "Intragovernmental Debt Holdings." It starts like this: "These intragovernmental debt holdings are eliminated in the consolidation of these financial statements." As of 2006, the total amount owed to these agencies was $3.66 trillion.

To find out what the real deficit is, just take the current year's national debt and subtract the previous year's national debt from it. Then add the increase of intragovernmental debt, and the increase in future liabilities that they conveniently forgot to fund, and there you are . . . the real deficit. This is what should be reported to the public. Unfortunately, it isn't.

When you calculate the deficit by actually figuring out just how far into the hole we go each year, you'll find that it's usually somewhere between two to three times higher than what the government reports. When you use generally accepted accounting principles (GAAP), the standard to which all public companies are held), which includes future liabilities, our national debt is some twenty times higher than the government tells us. Using this formula, the true deficit for fiscal year ending 2007 stands at some $4 trillion.

Listen to the Prophets, and Profit

Robert Kiyosaki points out that when Social Security was created in 1935 there were 42 workers for every retiree, whereas today there are 3.3, and by 2030 there will be only 2. This is a by-product of the aging of the baby boomer generation. Another effect it will have on your finances is that the same law that created the Individual Retirement Account (IRA) also mandates that the biggest stock market crash in history is yet to come, because as the baby boomers begin to retire, they will be required to pull money out of their IRAs, which will result in high stock sales volumes and not enough demand for the stocks being sold. And that's about as basic as economics gets: High supply and low demand equals falling prices. Every investor should read *Rich Dad's Prophecy* by Robert Kiyosaki and Sharon Lechter because it provides valuable insight into how the retiring baby boomers will significantly affect your financial future. I highly recommend it; in fact, if you want to survive what's coming, it's mandatory.

Another person who has a deep understanding of the subject is Congressman Ron Paul. He's a ten-term congressman whose passion is monetary policy. Since 1976, he's been on nearly every banking committee and monetary commission.

I had the honor of interviewing the congressman at length (you can see it at GoldSilver.com). I asked him some very tough questions about the economy, and he answered with an honesty and candor that was astonishing. Here's what he said about the unfunded liabilities of the United States:

This is so huge that nobody can quite comprehend it. It is into the many, many trillions of dollars. All we know for certain is that it's not workable and it will fall apart.

I always tell the elderly, "You are always going to get a check. We are always going to send you a check for your Social Security, and it's always going to go up. But we will always fudge on what the real rate of inflation is . . . so your real income is going to stay flat or go down. You're always going to get a check, but the question is: What's it going to buy? If electricity doubles, and your check doesn't double, you're going to suffer."

I think this country is going to get much, much poorer and the entitlements will finally have to end because just printing the money and running up the deficit or expecting foreigners to continue to loan us the money is not going to last. It's just a dream, and it's very, very serious.

Wow! Now that's telling it like it is.

The China Shop

Most people think that the United States is borrowing most of the world's savings to fund the deficit. Ben Bernanke, our Fed chief, who is presiding over ever higher inflation rates, even made a speech in 2005 titled "The Global Saving Glut and the U.S. Current Account Deficit." The speech makes it sound as if the rest of the world has way too much savings, so much so that they don't know what to do with it except loan it to the U.S.

People think that the excess dollars that go overseas due to the U.S. trade deficit are being loaned back to us. This is not entirely true. To be sure, there is a lot of real foreign investment happening in the United States, but it's not nearly to the extent reported. So where does all that extra currency that purchases all those U.S. Treasury Bills to fund a large part of the deficit come from? The countries that are the U.S.'s major trading partners create it.

China is the best example, so we'll start there. When someone in the U.S. buys something in the U.S. that was made in China, that vendor bought that product from a Chinese businessman and paid in U.S. dollars. The Chinese businessman then deposits those dollars into his checking account at his local Chinese bank. The bank then converts the dollars to yuan. Now the local bank has a glut of dollars and a shortage of yuan, so it sells the extra dollars to the People's Bank of China (PBC) and buys more yuan.

As long as the trade between the two countries is in equilibrium there is no problem. But when one country is running continuous trade deficits and the other continuous surpluses, as the United States and China currently are, a problem arises.

In the case of China, because there is more currency flowing into China than out, the PBC ends up with a huge glut of U.S. dollars. Under the rules of the game of international trade and currency exchange they are supposed to sell those excess dollars on the Forex (foreign exchange market) and buy yuan. But that would mean that there would be a glut of dollars and a shortage of yuan, which would cause the dollar to fall and the yuan to rise. Chinese goods would then become very expensive in the U.S., slowing China's exports, and that's the last thing China wants.

So, to get around the international trade and currency exchange game, China bends the rules. The PBC takes the extra dollars and neutralizes them by buying a dollar-denominated asset, most often some sort of interest-bearing investment instrument, like U.S. Treasuries. This keeps the yuan from rising and the dollar from falling.

This is known as "neutralizing" or "sterilizing" excess currency inflows. The funny thing is that the U.S. was doing the same thing by sterilizing excess gold inflows all through the 1920s to keep the dollar artificially low and exports up, and it was one of the major factors that contributed to the Great Depression.

So, if the PBC used the excess dollars to buy U.S. Treasuries, and didn't buy the yuan on the Forex to sell to the businessman's local bank, where did the PBC get the yuan? Richard Duncan, in his excellent book *The Dollar Crisis*, explains it this way:

> There is a widespread misconception that the United States relies on the savings of other countries to finance its current account deficit. This is incorrect. During recent years, at least, the U.S. current account deficit has been financed primarily by money created by the central banks of other countries.
>
> Therefore, it is not a matter of the U.S. using up all the rest of the world's savings to fund its deficit. It is a matter of that deficit being financed by the central banks of the United States' trading partners. And, for their part, Asian central banks, in particular, have consistently demonstrated their ability and willingness to create money in order to finance the U.S. current account deficit.

As I said, the U.S. was sterilizing excess money inflows in the 1920s, just as China sterilizes excess currency inflows today, so history is repeating itself. It's the same game but with a little twist. Well, actually it's a really big twist. When Europe paid the U.S. in gold, the Federal Reserve would cheat gold by locking it away instead of expanding the currency supply to match, thereby preventing the commensurate inflation it would have caused, keeping the price of U.S. goods low, and insuring a continuing trade surplus. This was hugely deflationary. As the rest of the world bought cheap American goods, gold would just disappear into the black hole of the Federal Reserve and the world money supply would contract.

When China sterilizes excess currency inflows, however, it's extremely inflationary. For every excess dollar that China neutralizes by buying U.S. Treasuries, the PBC has to conjure up a commensurate amount of yuan out of thin air. This is brand-new currency, commonly called "high-powered money" because when it hits the commercial banks it is used as the reserve asset for fractional reserve banking. If you recall the chapter on the Federal Reserve, fractional reserve banking means that when someone deposits one dollar in the bank, the bank can keep that dollar in reserve to pay out against deposits, and (under a 10 percent reserve) they are allowed to create $9 in loans. I like to call it "bunny money," because it multiplies like rabbits.

For more than two decades the inflation of China's currency supply has puffed up their financial, stock market, and manufacturing sectors, but now it is finally with down to the consumer level. Price inflation is heating up bigtime, with workers complaining about the cost of living, and causing Beijing to ask local governments to raise minimum wages, which is a cost that companies will have to pass on to consumers in the form of higher prices, which will cause workers to complain about the cost of living, and so on. But the increase in prices that were caused by the inflation of its currency supply isn't just a local problem within China. Soon, one of China's leading exports to the world is expected to be price inflation itself.

I recently interviewed a job applicant who, along with her husband, has owned a successful import business since 1983, which imported goods mostly from China. But lately they've received numerous price increases, the most recent coming so soon on the heels of the last that new price sheets hadn't even been printed reflecting the previous prices. Because of the new higher prices, their goods aren't as competitive, so now she's looking for a job. As Ben Simpfendorfer, China strategist for the Royal Bank of Scotland, puts it, "Where China was a deflationary influence over the last ten years, it will be an inflationary influence over the next ten years."

All this is the free markets, once again winning out over our government's meddling and correcting the imbalances. China pegged its currency low to keep exports cheap. To maintain the low peg it had to create currency. The extra currency is causing the cost of living to increase. Increased worker's pay causes the cost of Chinese goods, whether consumed domestically or exported, to rise. Then the increased price of Chinese goods in the U.S. causes U.S. consumers to buy less of them. And this will continue until the trade imbalance is corrected.

As a result of all the games that can be played under a fiat currency system, the total cumulative U.S. trade deficit has grown to over $7 trillion since the dollar was taken off the gold standard in 1971 (Chart 21). These deficits are sustained by fiat currency from other central banks around the world. All

Chart 21. U.S. Trade Balance

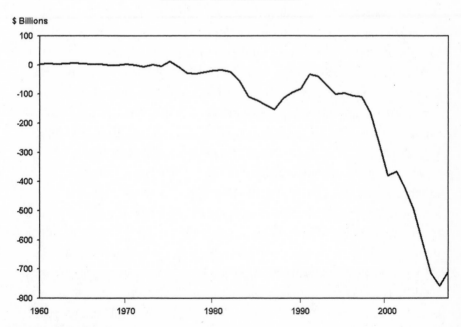

Source: U.S. Census Bureau

the while, these banks are hoarding ever increasing mountains of U.S. debt (Treasuries) and artificially propping up the value of the dollar. Much of our debt cannot be repaid, and if our trade partners begin to dump U.S. Treasuries on the world markets, the whole credit bubble will implode, resulting in a worldwide depression. The longer governments and central banks try to cheat the free markets, the greater the pain will be when the correction occurs. Like the precious metals, the free markets always win.

Japan's Money Bomb

There is another way that a country can keep their exports high and their currency values low. In 2003, Japan's economy was in shambles and suffering a long, slow, and grinding deflation it couldn't get out of since its 1989 stock market crash. In an effort to turn the economic tide, Japan embarked on one of the grandest currency creation experiments since World War II. In November of 2002, then Fed governor Ben Bernanke, whose academic research when he was a professor of economics at Princeton was on Japan's recessionary woes, gave his now infamous speech about dropping money from helicopters if need be to prevent an economic downturn such as the one Japan experienced.

In January of 2003, Japan actually took his advice. Over the next fifteen months the Japanese created 35 trillion yen, which they used to buy 320 billion U.S. dollars, pushing the yen down, and the dollar up, and keeping their exports to the U.S. artificially low. They then used those yen to buy U.S. Treasuries. This jump-started Japan's economy, and lifted the U.S. out of one of the shortest recessions on record (the 2001–2003 recession) and into its largest real estate bubble in history. U.S. interest rates fell to historic lows, credit was cheap, and people began to buy houses as investments in record numbers. I don't have to tell you how that ended. Chances are you're still feeling the effects today of the U.S. housing market crash and the mortgage-backed security meltdown. When all was said and done, Japan's economic money bomb amounted to one percent of global gross domestic product.

Once again, just like during World War I, the world currency supply is exploding. And some countries seem to be printing currency just for the heck of it. For instance, from April 2006 to April 2007 Russia's M2 money supply grew by 52.7 percent.

The International IOU

An often overlooked fact is that the bulk of the currency reserves in the world's central banks are not actually currency, but bonds, mostly in the form of U.S. Treasuries (U.S.-IOUs).

I used to have a hard time trying to comprehend the world monetary system. Chances are you find the system a bit mystifying as well. Thankfully, an analogy came to me one day that helped me connect the dots.

Picture a very large room. In this room are the heads of the U.S. Treasury, the Federal Reserve, the rest of the world's treasuries and central banks, all the world's commercial banks, and a bunch of hot-shot Wall Street elites. Then picture them all frantically making out IOUs and passing them back and forth to each other as fast as they can. That's the world's monetary system.

Now the foundation for this system is a bond issued by a country's Treasury, Ministry of Finance, or whatever they call it in their country . . . for now we're going to call it the government. These government bonds are the foundation bonds of the world's monetary system. Bonds basically say: "I owe you (IOU) X-amount of currency, plus X-amount of interest."

Many entities buy these government bonds. But when a country wants to create some currency, the government sells a bond to their central bank. The central bank writes a check against a zero balance in their checking account for however many dollars, euros, yen, or whatever the government wants, and it buys the bond. The currency has now sprung into existence, and later can be used to redeem the bond. Therefore, the bond is an IOU for the currency. But since the currency is also a claim check to redeem the bond when it matures, the currency is an IOU for the bond. Get it? No, me neither. That's because it's crazy. If you or I did this, we'd be accused of fraud.

The government now circulates the currency by paying people and buying stuff. People deposit currency into the banks, so the banks and other entities end up with lots of currency. When a person wants to buy a house, they go to the bank and take out a loan by signing a mortgage. The mortgage also says: "IOU X-amount of currency, plus X-amount of interest." The bank creates a book entry for the amount of currency you borrowed and at the same time, a book entry is made as a debt that you owe on your loan account. On the bank's balance sheet, liabilities are netted out against assets, the books stay balanced, and the bank is happy. But the bank didn't loan you any of the currency it had on hand. It just created book entries. When you signed that mortgage the currency that the bank loaned to you sprang into existence the second your pen hit that paper. The bank just expanded the world's currency supply.

Mortgage-Backed Securities and the Derivatives Monster

The bank then takes a bunch of mortgages and packages them up into a bond (IOU) called a mortgage-backed security (MBS). You've probably heard about those in the news lately. They are largely responsible for the subprime mortgage mess. Mortgage-backed securities are complicated financial tools (what I like to call "financial voodoo") created to limit financial institutions' risk when it came to debt. But instead of limiting the risk, they have spread the risk to the entire world. Whenever a bank gives you a loan for a house, it rarely keeps that loan. Rather, it sells it to Wall Street, who then packages it and other loans into MBS and sells them to investors worldwide. Now foreclosures in Las Vegas, Nevada, can cause a town to go bankrupt in Norway.

Our current mess stems from the fact that the Fed kept interest rates so low, for so long, that it caused an immense wave of currency and credit creation, which devalued the dollar and caused housing prices to rise at record levels. With credit so cheap, and currency so plentiful, soon banks were loaning money to any bum who walked off the street as long as he combed his hair. The banks then sold those mortgages to Wall Street, and those geniuses packaged the loans, both standard and subprime, into MBS and sold them off to investors.

Because banks were reckless in their lending standards, they gave loans to people for houses they couldn't afford. Suddenly feeling rich, those people pulled money out of their houses as if they were ATMs and spent it, often on depreciating items like televisions or cars. Then something totally unexpected happened (at least to those who were punch-drunk on cheap money). The expected rate adjustments that were clearly spelled out in the loan documents came due, and suddenly people couldn't make their payments. You know what happens next. A rash of foreclosures at record levels caused mortgage-backed securities to fail. People lost a lot of money and the government tried to bail them out. In the meantime, the financial institutions panicked and credit dried up.

Mortgage-backed securities are part of what I like to call the derivatives monster. Derivatives are financial instruments whose price and value are derived from the value of the assets underlying them, like the real estate underlying MBS.

Derivatives *may* be the single largest threat to the world's financial system. And they are definitely one of the darker clouds in the coming storm. I say *may* be because the potential problems and risks are so well hidden that we have no idea how much havoc they might wreak. The vast majority of them are created over the counter, through private agreements instead of being traded through an exchange. That means that they are not subject to the standardization and regulation of an official body like the Securities and Exchange Commission (SEC). Derivatives make up the world's largest financial market. In 2008 derivatives more than doubled and now exceed a quadrillion dollars, or about twenty times the global gross domestic product.

The Daisy Chain

Many derivatives have an expiration date; so, before a derivative expires, a new derivative contract will be placed on top of it, involving new parties. This process is referred to as daisy chaining.

Eventually, someone in a contract might feel that a change in circumstances has placed his bet at greater risk, so he'll make another bet in the opposite direction to limit his risk. The biggest problem is that no one knows who might be at the end of a derivatives chain. It could be a bankrupt corporation in Panama that is unable to pay up. If so, then a domino effect happens, with each party not being able to pay the next.

Something similar to this almost happened in 1998 when a highly leveraged hedge fund called Long Term Capital Management (LTCM) had a stroke of bad luck. From its inception, LTCM was something special. Its board was made up of the most respected golden boys of Wall Street, and the two economists that shared the Nobel Prize in economics for developing the mathematic formulas for calculating the risk/price of options and minimizing risks in investing.

As I said, LTCM was highly leveraged, with only $4 billion in assets but over $1.25 *trillion* in derivatives bets (equal to the annual U.S. budget at the time). In the summer of 1998, a set of unusual geopolitical circumstances caused LTCM's Nobel Prize–winning formula to fail. In 1997, Thailand had a currency crisis when the free markets overwhelmed the government's peg to the dollar, causing a massive devaluation of the Thai baht, which then caused the country's stock market to crash. The resulting tsunami of economic crisis known as the Asian Contagion took down virtually every economy and stock market in Southeast Asia (with the exception of Japan), thus bringing to a close what was known as the Asian miracle. Then in 1998, Russia lost control of their currency peg, the ruble crashed, and it defaulted on its international loans. All this economic turmoil caused LTCM's bets to turn bad, and its assets shrank from $4 billion to just $600 million against the $1.25 trillion in bets. As the threat of insolvency loomed, the domino effect I talked about earlier became a real possibility. The Federal Reserve Bank of New York arranged a bailout by putting together a consortium of leading investment and commercial banks to buy the fund and unwind its bets.

Most of the public never knew that the world's financial system came within a few days of freezing up. It's not a matter of *if* something like this can happen again. Rather, it's a matter of *when*. And next time there might not be a bailout. Warren Buffett, the world's most successful investor, sums up the dangers of derivatives nicely: "The derivatives genie is now well out of the bottle, and these instruments will almost certainly multiply in variety and number until some event makes their toxicity clear. Central banks and governments have so far found no effective way to control, or even monitor, the risks posed by these contracts. In my view, derivatives are financial weapons of mass destruction, carrying dangers that, while now latent, are potentially lethal."

The failure of Long Term Capital Management was considered too hazardous to the world economy not to bail out. Now the Federal Reserve and the rest of the world's central banks are bailing out the subprime mortgage sector.

Here's an example. It started in the summer 2007 when the problems with the subprime mortgage sector could no longer be concealed by the banking system, and the crisis finally made the news. In August the Fed cut rates 0.5

percent, and the European Central Bank (ECB) started injecting liquidity (currency in the form of cheap loans to banks). Later that month there were some small panic runs on branches of Countrywide Bank of California, the bank that wrote most of the subprime mortgages, as depositors demanded their currency. In September, the Fed cut rates 0.5 percent again. Then October saw bank runs across England when word got out that Northern Rock, the eighth largest bank in England, was in a credit crunch because of the MBS crisis and had to borrow from the Bank of England (England's central bank). As *USA Today* recounted "The most visible sign of economic jitters were the Depression era–like lines that formed outside Northern Rock's bank branches Friday morning after Northern Rock had gone to the Bank of England for an emergency loan to meet its obligations." The $80 billion bailout will cost British taxpayers some $1,500 per person.

That same month the Fed cut rates 0.25 percent and another 0.25 percent in December, and the Fed, the ECB, the Bank of England, and other central banks created another $40 billion of cheap credit, but it wasn't enough to halt the meltdown. So on December 19, 2007, the ECB injected another 350 billion euros into the economy, the equivalent of half a trillion U.S. dollars. In January the Fed cut rates 0.75 percent on the 22nd, and 0.5 percent on the 30th. Once again, the global currency supply is exploding.

Then on March 5, the Carlyle Capital Fund had a little problem when it found that some MBS it bought from Fannie Mae and Freddie Mac were pretty nearly worthless. That was the little problem; the big problem was that, like LTCM, this bet was highly leveraged, $31 of each $32 Carlyle had bet was borrowed.

Now trouble really started brewing. A good portion of that borrowed currency had come from Bear Stearns, which, coincidentally, was one of the major participators in packaging and selling MBS and was already in the process of taking huge losses on MBS they owned. On Wednesday, March 12, 2008, Carlyle announced that it was unable to pay the loans on its bets and that its creditors would be seizing all remaining assets.

Bear Sterns, being a major creditor, didn't need more MBS, and when word got out, the company collapsed. On Friday, March 14, as reported by *USA Today*, "Bear Stearns was crippled when market rumors began to swirl about the size of its exposure to mortgage-related securities, and whether it had ample reserves to cover potential losses. That led clients and investors to demand their money back, causing a run on the bank." The Fed did an emergency rate cut of 0.25 percent on Sunday, March 16 and another 0.75 percent cut on March 18. Finally, the Fed has arranged a wedding where J. P. Morgan Chase, which through mergers and acquisitions is probably the largest stockholder of the Federal Reserve, will gain control of Bear Stearns at 95 percent off its price from the year before.

But the story gets even better! The Fed will buy the worst of Bear Stearns MBS before Morgan takes over. And it'll cost us, the U.S. taxpayer, another $30 billion.

Bear Stearns is only the beginning. Bailouts like these will get bigger and become more frequent, thus causing the currency supply to expand, and thereby lowering the value of your hard-earned cash.

The Currency Game

I hate to tell you this, but the currency system is stacked against you. If you are an average American who works hard and saves your cash in the bank, you are the biggest loser in this system. The biggest winners are the financial sectors that create the new currency. They grow richer as you grow poorer.

The reason the financial sector is so wealthy is simple. Whenever anyone counterfeits currency (whether illegally, or in the case of the banking system, legally), value is effectively taken from the existing currency and transferred to the newly created currency. When new currency is created, its maximum purchasing power is conferred to its creator because it didn't cost the creator anything to make the currency. Even more, when the creator loans out the new currency it requires the return of the currency plus interest. So, the currency creator makes currency for nothing by stealing the value from your currency, and then loans out that currency to others and requires yet even more currency to be returned to them.

The borrower receives the second highest value from the units of currency because the currency is not yet out in circulation until he buys something with it. Once he purchases something, however, the currency enters circulation and devalues the existing currency supply, which, as you've probably already guessed, makes prices for things like milk and gasoline rise. Now it's more expensive for you to purchase these items. The borrower of newly created currency gets more benefits than you from that currency precisely because he doesn't have to pay the price, so to speak. He purchases his goods with the borrowed money before the new currency has its effect on the currency supply. Thus, that is the concept of borrowing today and paying back tomorrow with cheaper dollars.

Savvy investors use this system to great advantage. Whether it is using margin in the stock market, or investing in real estate, the power of currency creation bestows great wealth transfer to those who use its leverage wisely. Borrowers who just finance their own home or car, and especially those who use cash-out refinancing, however, make themselves poorer by merely transferring their wealth from themselves to the bank.

Currency creation also is one of the ways an asset class can go from undervalued to overvalued. As the newly created currency enters a particular asset sector, let's say real estate, it causes that asset sector to inflate. People see the wave of wealth building and hop on, usually at the crest of the wave, right before it comes crashing down. In the process, enormous amounts of wealth are moved from other asset classes into the bubbling asset class. The asset classes where money is being withdrawn become undervalued, and savvy investors then begin to move money out of the inflated asset class back into the undervalued ones.

Is the system moral? No. But it is the system within which we live, and it confers great power to those who understand it and can manipulate it. The whole system is designed to transfer wealth from those who don't understand the system to those who do. As Congressman Ron Paul says, easy credit and the current fiat currency system are simply "a tax on the poor and the middle class."

The Convergence

In this chapter we have touched on the budget deficit, the unfunded liabilities, the trade imbalances, fractional reserve banking and the resulting explosion of the global currency supply, the derivatives monster that looms over us like the Death Star in *Star Wars*, and our faith-based financial system. All of these make up the dark economic clouds on our horizon today that will converge into the perfect economic storm tomorrow.

What I've covered in this chapter only scratches the surface. The problems and imbalances that the global financial system is facing could fill volumes. And all of this is happening at a time when terrorism threatens the world, U.S. foreign policy seems to be turning the opinion of the rest of the world against it, oil supplies are diminishing while half of the world's population is seeking the same level of prosperity (and energy usage) as the Western world, global warming is at our doorstep, and the U.S. government and most of its population has metaphorically maxed out their credit cards and now they think they're all going to retire and live off each other.

In uncertain times, investors around the world run for the perceived safety of government bonds. I believe, this time around, they will get slaughtered. When, not if, the credit worthiness of the U.S. government is downgraded, their bonds, just like the MBS bonds, will be sold at huge discounts, and any investor holding them will lose, just as they did in the 1970s and 1980s when bonds were nicknamed "certificates of wealth confiscation." How quickly we forget.

Remember our wise old farmer from earlier in the book? When he knows a storm is coming, he moves his cows to safety and prepares for the worst. We need to do the same thing financially. While the coming storm will have horrible repercussions for those who are financially unintelligent, it's great news for precious metals investors. Now I'm not saying we should stand by and cheer on our politicians as they waste our tax dollars and make promises they can't possibly deliver on. But it does seem that Washington refuses to learn from history, and is intent on following its suicidal path to its end.

I'm trying to do what I can to stop them. I raise my voice in protest. I write my congressman. And I wrote this book. But if I can't stop them, I'm going to make darn sure that I have not only protected myself from the politicians' stupidity, but also have capitalized on it. Because every dollar wasted and every new dollar printed expands the global supply of every type of currency except two. Gold and silver are the only currencies they can't print.

History always repeats itself. When a civilization debases its currency supply, all that currency will once again come chasing that same tiny little pile of metal, and gold and silver will revalue themselves measured in those currencies. This will happen to the United States, just as it did to every empire in history. Those who recognize this stand to become wealthy beyond belief.

Chapter 9

The Perfect Economic Storm

In the last chapter I talked about the coming economic storm. I believe it will be the perfect storm, and there isn't anything we can do to stop it. Events are forming that, once fully converged, will result in quick and devastating economic destruction. The effects might not be as breathtakingly awesome as nature's destruction, but the destruction will be real nonetheless. And if you think the government will help you, you are sorely mistaken.

Our political system is structured to punish anyone who thinks about, or makes plans for, anything further than four years into the future. These days the only way a politician can get elected is by promising more free stuff than the politician he is running against. But the public doesn't seem to realize that the free stuff isn't really free.

It would be political suicide for a politician to even suggest that we should cut back in any area of the budget. If you suggest cutting the military budget, the right wing will tell you you're un-American and there are terrorists under your bed. If you suggest cutting Social Security, AARP will mobilize their tsunami of voters against you. And if you suggest cutting Medicare and Medicaid, the entire population will rise up against you screaming, "But health care is the single most important issue of our day."

The problem is that every issue is the single most important issue of our day. That is why the tough choices that need to be made to shore up our economy won't be made.

To this you must add the fact that we have essentially become a socialist society living under the delusion that we are still free market capitalists. We forget that we are the government. The government isn't some benevolent, separate entity with unlimited deep pockets. Whenever a problem arises, the majority always says the same thing, "The government should do something about it." They all seem to think that our government should be everybody's safety net. When major hedge funds overleverage themselves, they think the government should bail them out, and when homeowners overmortgage their homes, they think the government should save them from foreclosure. We don't seem to make the connection that whenever the government "does something about it," it does so at half the efficiency and twice the cost of the private sector. Then it hands the public the bill through either direct taxation, or through inflation taxation. That means, in the end, we all pay.

One of the biggest problems is that we hire (i.e., vote for) the wrong people to decide how our currency is to be spent. I would venture to say 99 percent of the officials we send to Washington who are charged with the job of redistributing our wealth, and thus the task of running the economy, know nothing about economics. And if they do know, they don't really care because their term is only two, or four, or six years.

I believe we have passed the point of no return and all we can do now is radio in the conditions as they worsen and brace ourselves for the worst. George W. Bush as captain of the ship decided to sail us toward tax cuts, Medicare prescription drug benefits, and the war in Iraq. But unlike the captain of the *Titanic*, he's not going down with the ship. We are.

There is a fiscal flood of biblical proportions coming. You may think our economy is a big enough boat to weather the storm. It's not. As much as I would like to see the entire boat saved, it just won't happen. It will be every man and woman for themselves. The good news is you can still save yourself and your family.

In their 2002 book, *Rich Dad's Prophecy*, Robert Kiyosaki and Sharon

Lechter provide insights on how to build your own ark, so you can safely sail through the coming flood caused by the government's reckless economic policies. If you read that book, you know the predictions they made in 2002 are beginning to come true today. As I've said, if you haven't read the book, you need to: It's absolutely required reading for any investor who wishes to weather the storm.

One of the best ways to protect yourself from the coming economic storm is to transfer your wealth into asset classes that will hold the tide. The best asset class, in my opinion, is the topic of this book—precious metals. The rest of this chapter will be devoted to showing you why precious metals will provide a safe harbor for any investor who wishes to moor their wealth to them.

Big Government and Inflation

The biggest problem facing America is really big government. It's a monster that needs continuous feeding. Before Roosevelt's New Deal, the federal government was 3 percent of the economy; today it's over 26 percent. And when you add in state and local governments, plus the cost of regulatory compliance, plus the cost of all of the business that provides the goods and services that support all of the government agencies, it's more than 50 percent of the U.S. economy.

I believe the biggest thing to worry about in the coming storm is government coming to the rescue. And with the government so big, and so pervasive, and with everyone expecting government to provide a safety net for every possible contingency . . . it will. In fact, as you have read in the last chapter, it's already begun. This application of our government was never intended. As noted economist Milton Friedman puts it, "Government has three primary functions. It should provide for military defense of the nation. It should enforce contracts between individuals. It should protect citizens against crimes against themselves or their property. When government—in pursuit of good intentions—tries to rearrange the economy, legislate morality, or help special interests, the costs come in inefficiency, lack of innovation, and loss of freedom. Government should be a referee, not an active player."

People don't realize what government bailouts of private financial institutions really cost. The savings and loan crisis of the late 1980s cost taxpayers

$150 billion. In 1989 the U.S. population was less than 250 million. That means everyone in the U.S. paid more than $600 each ($1,000 in 2007 dollars), either through taxes or inflation, to fix problems stemming from those financial institutions' stupidity. But that's nothing compared to what lies ahead.

The reason the potential for systemic financial failure of our economy exists at all is because the public allowed themselves to be hoodwinked by big banks and big governments. It was a process that took a few hundred years to unfold. The first con job we allowed ourselves to be taken in by was fractional reserve banking. The second con job was allowing fractional reserve banks to be pyramided on top of fractional reserve central banks. The third big mistake was not rising up against our government and the central banks in 1971 when the Federal Reserve, in collusion with President Nixon, made the U.S. dollar into a purely fiat currency. The result is inflation, inflation, and more inflation. (For a fuller understanding of the subject, I recommend *The Case Against the Fed* by Murray N. Rothbard.)

Many economists, financial advisors, and money managers feel that all the financial disequilibria created by the dollar standard, U.S. budget and balance of trade deficits, and currency creation by the central banks are building up and storing energy that will one day result in an enormous wealth transfer. Will the transfer come gradually, or will it spring upon us suddenly? Some believe it will be sudden, triggered by an event, rather than a slow meltdown. Whatever form this transfer takes, those who had the foresight to move their wealth to the safe harbors of gold, silver, and precious metals will reap the benefits.

There is, however, disagreement among economists as to whether the result will be deflation, inflation, stagflation, or hyperinflation.

Deflation is a contraction of the currency supply, which causes the currency to gain value and prices to fall. Deflation can happen rapidly, as in the case of the Great Depression, or slowly, as in the case of Japan in the 1990s.

Inflation is a mild increase in the currency supply, which causes the currency to lose value slowly and prices to rise.

Stagflation is economic stagnation, where the economy might be in a recession and just can't seem to get going, combined with high unemployment and high price inflation as in the 1970s.

Hyperinflation is inflation on steroids. There's no exact definition of the

point where big inflation turns into hyperinflation. Some say it's when inflation reaches 20 percent to 30 percent monthly. I like to think of it as the point
where confidence in the currency is falling faster than the currency can be
printed, and therefore the total value of the currency supply contracts regardless of how fast the total quantity of currency is increased. The International Accounting Standards Committee says it's when cumulative inflation
approaches or exceeds 100 percent over a three-year period. That's only 26
percent annual inflation, and we're already inflating the currency supply at 18
percent. But the definition I like best is from John Williams, who says it's when
"the largest pre-hyperinflation bank note ($100 bill in the United States) be-
comes worth more as functional toilet paper/tissue than as currency."

So let's run through a few scenarios to see how gold and silver should
perform.

Before I start, however, I'd like you to keep this mantra at the forefront
of your mind as you read this next section:

There is no possible scenario in which gold and silver do not rise.

Follow the Yellow Brick Road

SCENARIO #1: MILD INFLATION (THINGS GO ALONG PRETTY MUCH JUST AS THEY ARE)

I believe this is the least likely scenario. There is way too much economic
disequilibrium in the world for things to just continue, and even Ben
Bernanke agrees: "The large U.S. current account deficit cannot persist in-
definitely because the ability of the United States to make debt service payments and the willingness of foreigners to hold U.S. assets in their portfolios
are both limited."

In other words, we buy stuff from everybody else, then everybody buys
IOUs in the form of U.S. Treasuries, corporate bonds, mortgage-backed securities, and hard assets such as companies, stock (partial ownership) in companies, real estate, and such. America buys stuff from the rest of the world by
selling them pieces of America . . . and it's a very, very serious problem.

I've already shown throughout this book how deep and how wide the U.S.
trade imbalance problem is. The reason I believe moderate inflation is the

least likely result of these imbalances is because eventually the world will lose confidence in the U.S. dollar. On that day, they will want to cash in on all the U.S. Treasuries they own. Unfortunately, we won't have the currency to pay up, so will have to print it. Whatever effect this will have on our dollar, and on the world economy, you can bet it won't be steady-as-she-goes, moderate inflation.

So, out of all the possible scenarios, I believe the status quo is the only scenario that is pretty much impossible. But even if all I've just described doesn't happen, and we go along just as we are, it means the global currency supply will continue its exponential rate of growth, and thus the value (purchasing power) of all currencies will continue to fall. All currencies, that is, except two, the only currencies they can't print: gold and silver. Currently, those currencies are severely undervalued. Mark my words, gold and silver will catch up, and then some.

SCENARIO #2: DEFLATION

This is Ben Bernanke's greatest fear. I've read his book *Essays on the Great Depression* and many of his speeches. Generally, once you've read a little of Bernanke's work, you come away with the feeling that, if we experience deflation, it'll be short-lived.

So why is the Fed so terrified of deflation? Because an IOU-based monetary system carries with it the inherent risk of complete and utter implosion. To find the answer, we only need to study our own history, namely, the Great Depression.

Debt can become excruciating in a deflation. In the words of our own Ben Bernanke: "The seriousness of the problem in the Great Depression was due not only to the extent of the deflation, but also to the large and broad-based expansion of inside debt in the 1920's."

It works like this. Let's say your income is $100 per month, and your debt payments are $40 per month (mortgage, car, and credit card payments), and you now have $60 left. With $50 you can pay for your utilities, insurance, food, gasoline, and have $10 of disposable income for dinner and a movie. Life is pretty good.

But in a deflation just about everything declines, including wages, prices, gross domestic product, and the money supply, but most importantly for you, your income. In the Great Depression nominal income fell by 53 percent. Using my earlier example, your monthly income would now be $47, instead of $100. You might be thinking to yourself, *Yeah, but aren't prices falling too? So my purchasing power stays the same?* Well, yes and no. Even though prices are falling to match income, debt isn't; it's nominal, which means it's a fixed number. So your debt payments are still $40 but your income is now $47. You can forget about the movie, the gas in your tank, and your insurance . . . you can even forget about your utilities, because all you've got left after servicing your debt is $7, and you're going to need that to eat.

Now you have to sell the house, but you still owe $5,000 on it and you find out that it's only worth $2,000. You stand by in utter disbelief as your home is foreclosed on, your car repossessed, your furniture auctioned, and the courts distribute any savings you had to your creditors. After working all your life, you are homeless and on the street.

Chart 22 is the ratio of debt to GDP, in other words, how much debt there was in the country as a percentage of (or compared to) the level of all the goods and services produced in this country (gross domestic product).

Chart 22. Credit Market Debt as a % of GDP

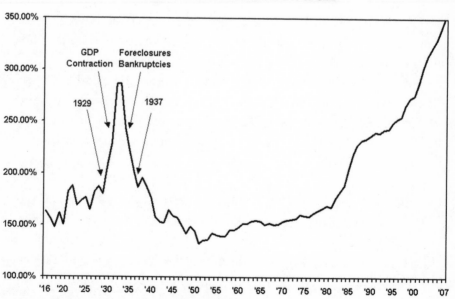

Source: Federal Reserve, Bureau of Economic Analysis, U.S. Census Dept.

When the stock market crashed in 1929, the GDP shrank, so even though no one took on new debt, debt as a percentage of GDP grew from 180 percent to 280 percent as the economy slid into the depths of the Great Depression in just a few short years.

Then, debt levels plunged from 1933 to 1937, while GDP grew only slightly. In human terms, that plunging line meant the loss of the family farm that had been handed down from generation to generation. That line that is falling from 1933 to 1937 statistically represents foreclosures, bankruptcies, and the liquidation of bad loans. But behind the statistics were real human beings who were watching their lives being destroyed.

That huge contraction of the currency supply happened in a time when our monetary system had a foundation of real money: gold and silver, which couldn't evaporate into thin air. What could happen today, now that our entire monetary system is nothing but IOUs? An IOU only has value if the borrower has the ability to pay. You've probably already noticed that today our debt levels, as a percentage of GDP, are well above the historic levels of the Great Depression. In fact, as I write this, they are 350 percent of our national income. That makes the 180 percent we started out with in 1929 look warm and fuzzy.

Remember, in a deflation, the government suffers from the same problem of fixed debt and falling income (in the form of tax revenues) as the public does. Just as it does with the masses, this leads to insolvency.

In his speech "Deflation: Making Sure 'It' Doesn't Happen Here," Ben Bernanke famously talked about dropping money from helicopters. In the speech, he revealed just how far the Fed is prepared to go to prevent deflation. His solution is to keep throwing more and more currency, not money, at the problem. In the speech he talks of possibly lowering interest rates to zero percent.

Why am I spending so much time on problems in the economy, the deficit, trade imbalances, the unfunded liabilities, and statements from Ben Bernanke? Because the effect that they will have on gold and silver will be huge, and they are the largest factors driving the upcoming wealth transfer. So, if you want to understand why the value of gold and silver *must* rise, and why the wealth transfer *will* be so enormous, then you need to have an appreciation of the problems, and the government's lame efforts to fix them.

Ben Bernanke's and the Fed's potential solutions to deflation are very important. They reveal how terrified they are of deflation and the lengths they are prepared to go to prevent it. I've boiled down just the key points from one of Bernanke's speeches on how the Fed would create currency and pump it into the economy into just one paragraph. Let's take a closer look.

The Federal Reserve's broad-based proposals to fight inflation involve injecting money into the economy through purchases of assets. To prevent deflation, the Fed must expand the scale of its asset purchases or, possibly, expand the menu of assets that it buys. For example, mortgage-backed securities, corporate bonds, commercial paper, bank loans, mortgages, and foreign government debt, as well as domestic government debt. And they leave as a possibility the option of a broad-based tax cut, accommodated by a program of open-market purchases.

We'll just have to overlook the immorality of a private corporation (which is what the Fed is), that is not a part of any government, having the authority to buy up much of the world's assets with currency created from nothing. But, given the fact that the Fed would be bound and determined to prevent deflation regardless of the consequences, if deflation were to occur it would probably be short-lived. But what about its effect on gold and silver?

As you will see in later chapters, gold can make huge gains in purchasing power during a deflation. In fact, some of the best investments of the Depression were gold mining stocks. But this time around things are very different. During the Great Depression, gold and silver formed the basis of the world's monetary systems. This time they belong to no nation. They are separately traded currencies. While the world's central banks are frantically creating currency by buying each other's debt to stave off deflation, gold and silver remain the only currencies they can't print.

Also, this time around national economies are no longer separate islands as they were in the Great Depression. They are, in fact, global, and international investment is a major component. And finally, this time around, news and trades go everywhere and anywhere on the planet at the speed of light.

Therefore, if deflation takes hold in the United States, foreign investors will be looking at a slowing U.S. economy, and at corporate profits turning into losses as the indebtedness of most U.S. corporations turns against them. Thus, foreign investors will sell U.S. investments. Once investors have sold their dollar-denominated assets, they then have to exchange those dollars into their own currency by selling dollars and buying their own currency. This would cause the U.S. dollar index to fall, and precious metals to soar.

But what about U.S. bonds? Don't bonds do well in a deflation? Normally, yes. But the world is not facing normal economic conditions. In a deflation scenerio, the tax base shrinks dramatically. Today, the U.S. is heavily encumbered with debt and our deficit spending has run amok. So much so that the loss of tax revenues coupled with the fact that the entire world knows that the Fed will try to print their way out of deflation would cause the major credit rating agencies to downgrade the standing of U.S. debt. In fact, foreign investors don't even have to sell their U.S. debt to make the U.S. insolvent. All they have to do is stop buying.

Investors may, in the short term, run where they've been taught to run for safety and buy U.S. bonds in a kind of knee-jerk reaction. But think about it this way: Would you loan a guy your life savings and take his IOU, knowing that the guy is promising a rate of interest that's half the real rate of inflation, that he has been borrowing from everybody in town for more than seventy years, and that he has spent far more than he has borrowed for a majority of those years? I suspect not.

In this case, that "guy" is our very own government. The last time it paid back more than it borrowed was forty-seven years ago. It already owes more than five times its annual income through tax revenues. It's promised everybody in town that it will deliver goods and services to them that will cost it more than twenty times its annual income, even though it doesn't really have a dime to its name.

In the face of huge deflationary concerns, there would be precious few investment outlets for an investor to safely moor his portfolio. One of those harbors would be precious metals simply because, as I stated earlier, they are the one currency that cannot be printed by government fiat. As investors begin selling off their U.S. currency–denominated assets, which would continue the devaluation of the dollar, and began moving them into precious metals, the price would have to rise. It's pure and simple supply and demand. There's only so much gold and silver to go around, and the more demand there is, the higher their value will be.

SCENARIO #3: BIG INFLATION

If Bernanke were to achieve what I believe his true goal is—creating enough inflation to bring the real estate bubble in for a soft landing—this would require a much accelerated rate of inflation and real estate would experience an invisible crash, just like the Dow crash of 1966–1982 we talked about in previous chapters, as it reverts to an undervalued asset class. Under these conditions the price of real estate will stay flat or slowly rise. The expansion of the currency supply would be enormous compared to today, and the result would be that all other asset classes would rise faster than real estate, including, and especially, gold and silver.

Under big inflation all investments appear to rise, but many actually fall in value. This is simply due to the fact that while your investments might be returning 10 percent, the dollar would be inflating at 20 percent. Effectively, that would equate to a *loss* in value of 10 percent. That's why it pays to understand inflation and how it is the silent economic killer. In a situation like this, your best investments would end up being precious metals and commodities, because their prices would rise as the dollar inflated, and debt leveraged investments such as real estate, because you could borrow money at or below the cost of inflation, which means borrowing now and paying back with cheaper dollars later.

SCENARIO #4: HYPERINFLATION

If you read the history lesson at the beginning of this book, you will be familiar with the ravaging effects of hyperinflation. So there is no point in belaboring my point again. If hyperinflation were to occur in the U.S., the wealth transfer will be gargantuan.

Under hyperinflation all investments rise dramatically in price, and some gain in value, but all fall in value compared to gold and silver. In a hyperinflation, the one thing everyone needs is the one thing that is in the shortest supply, real money, and people will give you anything for it. Real estate, stocks, collectibles, businesses, and such, all will fall in value when compared to real money.

Again, your best investments would be precious metals, commodities, and debt-leveraged investments such as real estate. You will want a fixed, low-rate loan that you locked in before the hyperinflation. Then you'll be able to pay off your real estate with what would equate to a few minutes of work, now that you're getting paid ten million bucks an hour. If you do this, the bank ends up paying for your house, but you get to keep it.

But if you really want to get aggressive, as the price (not value) of your real estate soars, you could use your ever increasing equity to continually re-finance to acquire new properties. You'd probably want to stay leveraged to the max until you near the end of the hyperinflation . . . then pay it all off.

However, in a hyperinflation scenario there still will be nothing, and I mean nothing, that will even come close to the purchasing power gains of pre-cious metals.

Now repeat after me: *There is no possible scenario in which gold and sil-ver do not rise.*

Fortune-Telling

> *"The dollar standard is inherently flawed and increasingly unstable. Its demise is imminent. The only question is, will it be death by fire— hyperinflation—or death by ice—deflation? Fortunes will be made and lost, depending on the answer to that question."*

RICHARD DUNCAN, *THE DOLLAR CRISIS*

So how do I think things will play out? Let me tell you your fortune.

Many economists disagree as to whether our economy's demise will be caused by inflation or deflation. But, since Ben Bernanke became Fed chair-man, most economists, advisors, and newsletter writers who used to think we were headed for deflation have changed their mind and now think we're headed down the road to inflation. A number of them think it will be followed by a hyperinflation.

The only problem that I can see with this hypothesis is that I can't find an example anywhere in history of the public being richly rewarded for their stu-pidity. When everybody is on one side of the boat, the boat capsizes and sinks. Throughout history, whenever there is enormous financial upheaval and great wealth transfer, the wealth is always transferred to the big boys. The big boys always win. And if you look at the golden parachutes that all the executives that presided over our recent banking problems are getting you'll realize that, even when they lose, they win. Let me explain further what I mean.

When the real interest rate becomes negative (the interest rate is lower than the inflation rate), people take on excessive debt as well as excessive risk because that is exactly what the banking system is paying them to do.

The people of the United States have followed the lead of their government and adopted the same financial habits. The United States has a personal savings rate that is negative. Stephen Roach, managing director and chief economist at Morgan Stanley, says the U.S. savings rate is a record low for any leading global economic power in the history of the world. The only other time the personal savings rate was negative for so long was during the Great Depression.

Millions of families have maxed out their mortgages by using their homes as ATM machines and borrowing against them. Those families, and millions more, are also maxed out on credit card debt. Robert Kiyosaki teaches the difference between good debt and bad debt. Good debt works for you, bad debt works against you . . . this is bad debt.

Regardless of the size of your mortgage, at the end of a hyperinflation salaries go so high that you're able to pay off your mortgage in a short amount of time, possibly just a few minutes' worth of work. That means the bank ends up buying your house for you. I can't imagine the banks buying all those homes for Joe Sixpack and John Q. Public. No. In every instance I find in history, inflation happens to a nation of savers, and deflation happens to a nation of big spenders.

During World War I, inflation raged and everybody became spenders. The war ended and the U.S. went into the huge (but short-lived) depression of 1921. By the end of the Roaring Twenties, everyone had become big spenders, and then the biggest deflation in history, the Great Depression, happened. During World War II, everybody saved, expecting a deflation at the end of the war, and inflation happened. Even the conservative country of Japan became big spenders when their stock market and economy boomed, in what were their Roaring Eighties, and then deflation set in. It's kind of a damned-if-you-do, damned-if-you-don't sort of thing.

Do you remember when I told you about a guy who paid $1 million for a house just down the block from my friend's house? He put 20 percent

($200,000) down. Just a couple of years later the price of the house fell by 60 percent. The poor guy was underwater with an $800,000 mortgage at 12 percent interest on a house that, at its lowest point, appraised for only $400,000. It took him ten years to get back to the point where he could sell his house without a loss. Well, that real estate bubble was a micro-bubble compared to the one we are going through now.

I've been telling this story ever since the banks started offering the masses zero-down mortgages, and I've been asking, "What is tying homeowners to their homes this time?" What I've been expecting for several years is a recession (there have always been recessions, and there always will be).

In a recession, some people have to take pay cuts and some people get laid off. What happens when one of them just happens to be one of the millions of people who are up to their eyeballs in credit card and mortgage debt, and just barely able to make the payments? And then another? And another? The trickle of bankruptcies and foreclosures turns into storm clouds, which become a perfect storm.

Whenever things go really wrong in an economy there is an emotional backlash. First everyone wants to place blame. Second, they overreact with a knee-jerk response. Lending standards will be tightened, making the problem worse. As Peter Schiff, of Euro Pacific Capital, points out, "Home prices are a function of what future buyers can afford—not what past buyers paid. If new buyers are required to make 20 percent down payments, fully document their income, and fully amortize a fixed rate mortgage, they will not be able to pay nearly as much as what current owners paid during the bubble."

Soon the world will wake up to the fact that though the mortgage-backed securities are a big problem, there is an even bigger problem looming out there, the zero-down loan. MBS are the big problem for the financial sector. MBS only speed up the global transmission of problems through the banking sector. It's the zero-down loan that threatens to suck the world economy into a black hole.

In the end, I think we're in for a wild roller coaster of a ride, with a few whipsaws thrown in. First the threat of deflation, followed by a helicopter drop, followed by big inflation, followed by real deflation, and then followed by hyperinflation.

This scenario is the one that fulfills predictions made by Robert Kiyosaki, and several other people I have great respect for. I think that our current sub-prime fiasco will turn into a larger problem than it is now, and as the real estate sector begins to plummet, and the credit currency that was borrowed into existence begins to evaporate, the threat of deflation will loom. Then Ben Bernanke will come to the rescue and bail us out by orchestrating another helicopter drop of currency.

In his book *Rich Dad's Prophecy*, Robert Kiyosaki predicted that one of the greatest stock market booms in history was yet to come, and would last at least until 2007. This was amazing considering that the book was written back in 2002. The country was still reeling from 9/11 and financial scandals like Enron, while the Dow was finishing a three-year brutal bear market, and many analysts were predicting a bear market for many years to come. But Robert made his ultra-bullish prediction in the midst of all that bearish sentiment based on the fundamentals of the baby boom demographics and their retirement needs. The so-called experts called Robert a lunatic. Current events reveal he's a genius.

The day of reckoning will come when the millions of baby boomers reach the age where they have to take mandatory distributions from their IRAs. As they find that the investments they were counting on for their retirement, their homes and their IRAs full of mutual funds, have actually lost value, that the amount of stuff they can buy from the proceeds if they sell their home is actually less than when they bought their home. And as they realize their dream of comfortable retirement was just that, a dream, all those boomers will get scared and pull in their horns. They will stop spending. They will start selling off their assets. And Rich Dad's second prophecy, the greatest stock market crash in history, will unfold. More and more boomers will panic and sell. I believe this will also be accompanied by the greatest real estate crash the world has ever seen.

This perfect storm of bankruptcies and foreclosures will cause the currency supply to contract as the giant credit bubble pops, and all those big spenders become big savers. When people save their currency, it stops circulating. The economic engine runs out of oil and the whole thing locks up. This is Bernanke's worst nightmare. This is *real* deflation, and poor Ben is about to discover the true scale of the horrors of a credit bubble implosion.

When that happens, Ben "burn the currency" Bernanke will once again send out his armada of money-bomb-dropping helicopters, but this time something will be different. Something will have gone horribly wrong. The bombs will have been defused. The Fed will try pumping the banking sector by buying every kind of debt they can get their hands on, but to no avail. They will go to the extraordinary measures they had said they were prepared to go to. They will buy every mortgage, MBS, and any other type of debt that panicky investors and banks are trying to sell, but nothing good will come of it. They will start buying stocks to buoy the markets, but retail sales will continue to plunge. They will try broad-based tax cuts, but it won't jump-start the economy. They will work with foreign central banks to buy each other's debt, but the global economy will continue to plummet. People will finally see through the veil. They will see what Dorothy, the Scarecrow, the Lion, and the Tin Man saw. That the Wizard of Oz is really just a dopey old guy frantically pulling levers.

Remember when we talked about how during World War I the Germans increased their currency supply by 400 percent yet there was no price inflation because of the public's anxiety over the war and the uncertainty of their future? Imagine the anxiety 75 million baby boomers will feel as they approach retirement, only to find their homes and mutual funds are now worth next to nothing. The nest egg, ladies and gentlemen, has just cracked. When they get the tax rebates from Ben, are they going to buy that new big screen TV and the latest cell phone? I think not. I think they're going to save every dime they can get their hands on. Just like in Germany during the war.

But there will be a point at which a threshold is reached. For each income class it will be different. It will be the point were they feel they've finally got enough saved for retirement. For some it will be $100,000, for others it will be $1,000,000, and for others still it will be $10,000,000. Ben knows that there is a point where they'll finally feel safe enough to replace that aging computer, and maybe get that new TV. At this point the boys at the Fed will buy enough government debt to fund tax rebates for all the taxes paid in the previous year, but still nobody will buy that new car. The threshold the Fed is looking for will not be reached.

Then, in not so quiet desperation, Ben will say, "Screw the helicopters. Send in the bombers."

And as the shadows of millions of stealth currency bombers darken the skies, currency will begin to fall like rain in the desert. As Joe Sixpack and John Q. get tax rebate checks in the mail for all the taxes they paid during their entire lifetimes, fear will be temporarily alleviated and some of that currency will come out of hiding, just as in Weimar Germany. Prices will rise quickly and dramatically as all the stored-up currency energy is released. In a panic, "B2 Ben" (as I predict his new stealth bomber nickname will be) will call back the bombers, but it will be too late. There's nothing Ben will be able to do to stop it now, because the hyperinflation will have already begun. The Dow will begin an invisible crash of epic proportions, and gold prices will shoot to the moon. If you were wise enough to moor your boat in the safe harbors of gold, silver, and other commodities, you will weather the storm. It won't be pretty, but at least you'll be safe.

At this point, confidence in the currency will fall faster than it can be created. Cost of living increases for government employees and the cost of all government projects, the subcontractors, the labor, the materials, will all skyrocket. And each time more currency is created to pay for the increases, the value of the currency will fall even faster.

In times like that, governments have only two choices: shut down the government and all of its projects and services, send everybody home without pay, turn off the printing presses, and wait for the free market system to discover price levels that account for the quantity of currency in the supply; or print the currency into oblivion. Governments have always chosen the latter.

But the stored-up energy of excess currency creation doesn't have to take place within the United States, and it doesn't necessarily have to be in the future. In fact, there is an abundance of stored-up currency just waiting to be released right now. As I mentioned earlier, all the dollars we sent overseas to other countries to buy their goods are now sitting in their bank accounts, just waiting to be spent. Eventually, the world economy will lose faith in the U.S. dollar and will want to dump it by buying up goods. This will, of course, cause the price of those goods to rise, and could, and probably will, trigger a scenario much like the one I have just finished describing.

Throughout history economists have suffered from what I like to call "*this time* syndrome." *This time* they've become masters of the economic universe.

This time they've figured it out. *This time* they've tamed the economy. *This time* they've mastered the art of infinite currency amplification. *This time* a fiat currency will work!

History gives this a probability of zero. Each time we sailed toward economic doom the greatest financial minds in the world were at the helm. Do you really think we should continue letting them steer the ship?

Chapter 10

Coming in from the Cold . . . To Gold!

"Through the many economic debacles in human history runs one common thread: those who financially survive do so because they own gold."

MICHAEL J. KOSARES, *THE ABCS OF GOLD INVESTING*

Good Day Sunshine!

I promised you sunshine and now you're going to get it. The wealth transfer I talked about in the last chapter is real, and it is extremely powerful. During a cycle change, when one asset class is topping out while the other is bottoming out, the intensity of the wealth transfer that has already taken place does not go unnoticed. The herd sees that other people have made enormous gains, and they want some too. The public continues to chase yesterday's hot investment class, even though the big gains have already been made. The pronounced severity of the full transfer of wealth is only noticeable after the transfer is nearly complete . . . at the end of that cycle and the beginning of the new one. We'll talk a lot more about cycles in chapters yet to come, but this chapter is about the silver lining, and the silver lining (as you must have guessed by now) is precious metals, gold and especially silver.

The CPM Group is one of the leading commodities market research and consulting firms in the precious metals industry. It painstakingly gathers, compiles, and analyzes data on supply and demand and other forces that have an effect on precious metals prices. Their data for precious metals has been published annually since 1971 in their *Gold Yearbook* and *Silver Yearbook*, available at www.cpmgroup.com. Before writing this chapter I had the opportunity to interview CPM's founder and managing director, Jeff Christian. He believes that as long as there are increasing geopolitical and financial uncertainties in the world, gold and silver will continue to rise.

As we have seen, gold and silver do a periodic accounting of fiat currency creation. But to give you an idea of the scale of the move that gold and silver should do this time in bringing fiat currency to account, take a look at Chart 23, from the CPM Group's annual *Gold Yearbook*. It's the total dollar price of private bank deposits versus private gold holdings.

Chart 23. Private Bank Deposits vs. Gold Holdings

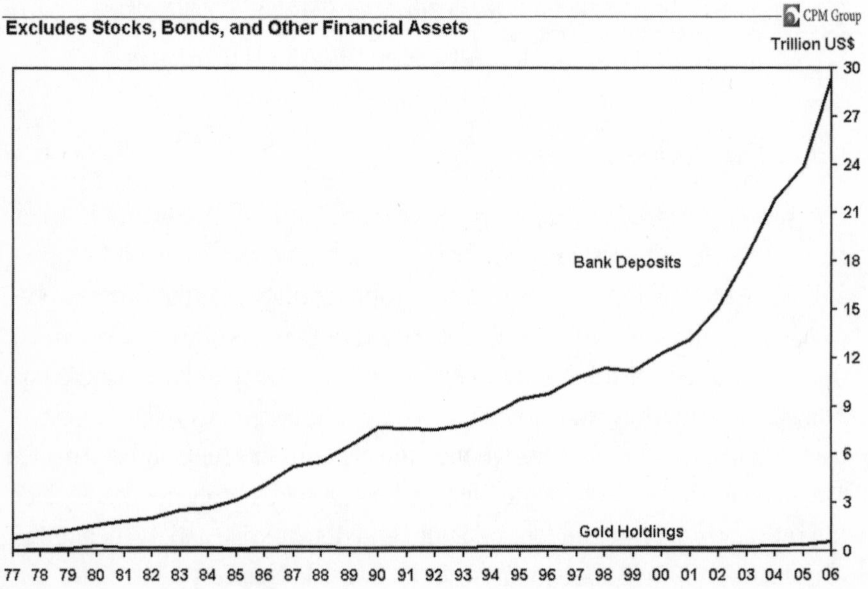

Excludes Stocks, Bonds, and Other Financial Assets

The bank deposits data for this chart was supplied to CPM Group by the Bank for International Settlements (BIS). Note that this chart excludes stocks, bonds, and other financial assets. Since they are private bank deposits, this chart also excludes official deposits such as government entities and central bank reserves. And, as the chart is of U.S. dollar–denominated deposits only, it also excludes all other currencies. So the financial instruments that are excluded from this chart absolutely dwarf U.S. dollar deposits. In other words, this chart is comparing only the tiniest fraction of financial instruments against privately held gold. That's a lot of dollars! What this chart reveals is that people have an immense amount of currency, but almost *no* money!

The dollar holdings make the current value of gold holdings look insignificant, at least at gold's current price. But that's about to change soon.

The free markets always balance these things out, and there are only three ways that can happen. Either the quantity of gold held by private investors has to increase by many, many, many times (an impossibility since there is only so much gold to go around), the quantity of dollars has to fall dramatically (possible, but not likely), or the scales will be balanced the same way they have always balanced—the masses will realize the loss of their purchasing power due to the ever expanding currency supply and lose faith in that currency. They will then come charging in, buying as much gold and silver as they can, bidding up the price of the only currencies that can't be printed, in order to account for all the currencies that can. And the markets will have caused that little gray line at the bottom of the chart titled "Gold Holdings" to rise up, accounting for the fiat currencies represented here by the black line titled "Bank Deposits," by changing gold's price.

Though this will be the greatest wealth transfer in history, it will be nothing more than a repeat performance of a play that governments, the public, and precious metals have been performing, time and again, since the play first premiered in Athens, circa 407 BC. The last performance was in the 1970s, but now it's playing again in a country near you. The actors may have changed, but the story remains the same.

Indeed, it may be coming sooner rather than later. The mass media is beginning to chatter more and more about the virtues of commodities investing, especially precious metals investing. Take for instance this article in the March 4, 2008, *Wall Street Journal* entitled, "Gold, Platinum Hit Record Highs"

Unlike oil, gold is still less than half its inflation-adjusted peak of $2,239.67, hit on Jan. 21, 1980. In January 1980, inflation was 13.9%, according to the U.S. Bureau of Labor Statistics. Today, inflation stands at 4.3%. "I would say we haven't seen the high for gold just yet," says Bart Melek, Global Commodity Strategist, BMO Capital Markets, in part because "inflation today is nowhere near as high as inflation during that period and investors will pile into gold if the inflation picture worsens."

At its peak during this time, gold's inflation-adjusted high using the CPI was $2,239.67. But as we already know, the CPI is the CP-Lie, so what was gold's 1980 high adjusted for inflation of the currency supply (Chart 24)? Well, as you know by now, that's a moving target because we don't know how many units of currency they're going to print. But, in 1980, M3 stood at about $1.8 trillion, and as I write this it is about $14 trillion. That means that as of April 2008, the U.S. currency supply is about 7.7 times larger than in January of 1980. So, adjusted for the expansion of the currency supply, the high that gold hit in January of 1980 was 6,611 2008 dollars! Coincidentally, in the 1970s gold rose from $35 to $850. That's a factor of 24.28 times. This time around we are coming off of gold's low of $252, set back in 2000–2001. If you take the low of $252 times 24.28 you get $6,118. And lastly, John Williams has an inflation calculator on his Web site that uses his reconstructed original CPI, and it says that the 1980 high of $850 equates to $6,484 as of April 2008.

So there you have it: $6,118 gold, $6,484 gold, or $6,611 gold. Take your pick.

Hallelujah!

The stock cycle peaked in 2000, so I moved the vast majority of my assets into precious metals by 2002. Shortly thereafter I started selling gold and silver. But back then, trying to get someone to buy gold at $300 per ounce was darn near impossible. It was like beating my head against a brick wall. The responses I got were "Gold is the dumbest investment anyone could make." "Gold has been losing money for twenty years." And my favorite, "What do you think I am? An idiot or something?" I remember thinking to myself, "Yes. Absolutely. Without a doubt." But now, with articles like the *Wall Street Journal* one just quoted, smart investors are bailing on their overvalued stocks

Chart 24. Inflation Adjusted Gold—2008 Dollars

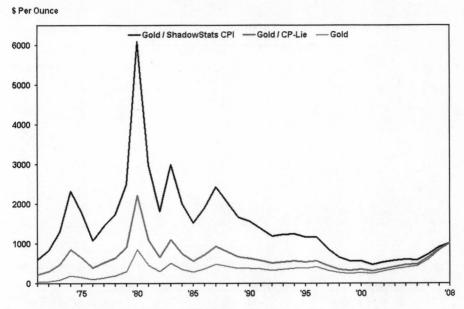

Source: Minneapolis Federal Reserve, ShadowStats.com

and bonds, and realizing just how much of a bargain gold is—and how wealthy it can make them.

Gold Rush!

Once again, smart investors know that the stock and bond markets have reached their peak, and have been declining for a while now. Those that are financially intelligent and in the know have been quietly moving their money into tangible assets, especially gold and silver. You may not have heard a lot about it in the mass media, but we are in the midst of the greatest gold rush in recorded history.

And as you can see in Chart 25, since 2000, investor purchases in gold have taken off like a rocket. So much so that private investors now own more gold than the world's central banks. On both an absolute, and on a percentage, basis, private investors have been buying far more gold in the greatest gold rush of all time, the gold rush of the twenty-first century, than they did in the gold

Chart 25. Central Bank Gold vs. Investor Gold

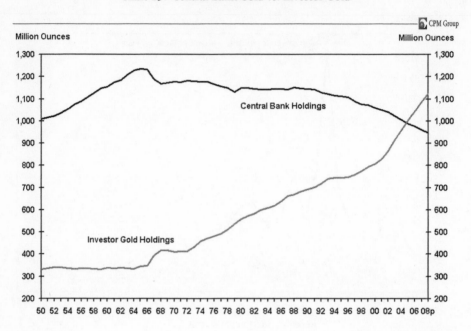

bull market of the 1970s. In fact, in the last five years investors have purchased almost three times more gold than in the five years from 1975 (when it once again became legal for Americans to own gold) to gold's price peak in January of 1980. This golden bull is still young, but it is bigger, brawnier, and more powerful than any golden bull the world has ever seen. Yet most of the world still seems blind to it. I am continually amazed at the staggering number of investors who lack vision enough to see it, even when someone like me is jumping up and down, screaming, pointing, and yelling, "Look . . . There it is!"

The amazing thing is, all this is happening in an environment of falling gold production. In fact, gold production has been shrinking for six of the past seven years. So where is all the gold that investors have been buying coming from? Well, things become really interesting, and a lot more fun, if you listen to the people who are considered the lunatic fringe of the gold sector: the lunatic conspiracy theorists known as the Gold Anti-Trust Action Committee (GATA).

GATA is a group of gold investors and professionals from the gold industry that includes mutual fund managers, commodities analysts, attorneys, precious metals dealers, and now even a few banks. GATA alleges that, with the cooperation of their governments, the world's central banks have been manipulating and depressing the price of gold. Why would the central banks want to keep a lid on the gold price? Because a rising gold price signals to the world that central banks are doing a terrible job.

What it comes down to is that governments and central banks will promise you this, and promise you that. But the only promise they can deliver on is the only promise they never say out loud: They *will* inflate the currency supply, and your currency *will* continue to lose value. They know the history of currencies, and they know that if the price of gold rises too fast, gold could attract the masses away from their fiat currencies. And just like every past example, their currencies would fail. So, it is in the governments' and central banks' best interest to have a falling gold price.

GATA has amassed an overwhelming body of evidence that shows that possibly 50 percent of the gold supposedly held in the world's central banks has been leased out to depress the price of gold. This is like an enormous short position against gold. I don't know about you, but as long as the central banks are going to subsidize my purchases of gold by depressing the price, I'm going to keep on buying.

If you take a close look at GATA's evidence you will see that it is on to something. I urge you to go to their Web site and check it out at gata.org.

In 1999, gold put in its all-time low against the Dow, and as I write this, it still takes 12 ounces of gold to buy one share of the Dow. It takes 350 ounces to buy a median-price, single-family home, but in 1980 it only took 68 ounces. In 2006, gold's value dropped to an all-time low against copper, and in 2007 it dropped to an all-time low against wheat.

The point of all this is to say that gold is cheaper than dirt right now, when compared to any other asset class, except dollars. And it'll probably still be cheap at $2,000, or even $5,000, per ounce. The only way to tell if it's cheap or expensive is to figure out how much stuff it can buy you. When it's buying you too much stuff, compared to historical averages, then, and only then, will it be expensive.

Chapter 11

The Silver Lining

You've heard that every cloud has a silver lining? Well, in this case the dark economic cloud does have a silver lining . . . literally. Because, monetarily, only gold and silver glitter. If you were excited by the prospects of investing in gold in the last chapter, wait till you get a load of the possible gains to be made by investing in silver.

Think You've Got Silver Pegged?

For the first 2,000 years that gold and silver were the primary form of money across the globe, the exchange rate between the two metals averaged 12 ounces of silver to 1 ounce of gold. In other words, silver's value was one twelfth that of gold. Of course, it would vary by region and time period. In China, during the Ming Dynasty, for instance, the exchange rate was 4 ounces of silver to 1 ounce of gold, and in ancient Egypt silver had the same value as gold; but, on the average, the ratio has been about 12 to 1.

It doesn't take a rocket scientist to figure out why. Gold and silver were money, circulating side by side, and the free markets balanced the scales. The ratio is set by the marketplace doing what it does naturally, which is discovering the fair price of something. This means that on average there was probably about twelve times more silver in circulation than gold throughout history. It is simply the market finding the price/quantity equilibrium based on the relative rarity of the two metals.

In the late 1800s Western silver discoveries and technological advances added significantly to supplies. This and other factors caused the value of silver to plummet to 1/100th of gold's value. Then, during the Depression, Franklin Roosevelt signed the Silver Purchase Act of 1934, and the U.S. began to amass the world's largest stockpile of silver. There were a few more silver purchases in the 1950s, and the stockpile peaked at 3.5 billion ounces.

But by the early 1960s silver's price had risen to $1.29 per ounce, not because silver was scarce, but because currency was too abundant. Silver was just catching up to the inflation of the currency supply. At $1.29 per ounce, the silver content in U.S. silver coinage equaled the face value of the silver coin. If silver's price were to rise any further, people could make a profit by going to the bank and getting a bunch of change, melting it down, and selling the silver. The government knew this and began selling silver to keep the price down.

For the first time ever, the public became net buyers of silver. The easiest way to buy silver was to take a paper dollar to the bank and ask for change. So much coinage was disappearing from circulation that the government was forced to remove silver from U.S. coinage beginning in 1965. The free market and the will of the public had once again forced the government's hand.

Throughout most of the 1970s silver's price ranged from $3 to $6, buoyed by Nixon's abolishment of the gold standard and an increase in the currency supply. Many investors sold much of their silver at a profit.

But in 1979, prices began to rise rapidly. People stopped selling silver, and for the second time in history the public became net buyers of silver. The first time the public became net buyers of silver it forced the government to discontinue the issuance of the last real money in the United States and replace it with copper and zinc tokens. This time, public buying of silver would cause the metal's price to explode to upward of $50 per ounce.

Get to the Point!

The reason I have given you all this background is because I think that investing in silver in the near future will be good as gold, or should I say, better. As I mentioned, when investors became net buyers of silver in the 1960s, it forced the government to abandon silver as money, and when investors became net buyers of silver in 1979, the price catapulted to over $50. Well, guess what? In 2006, for only the third time in history, the public became net buyers of silver once again.

As the CPM Group *Silver Yearbook* reported in 2007:

> Last year and this year represent major turning points in the silver market, years in which a tectonic shift in the silver investment demand occurs the likes of which are very rare. Specifically, investors shifted from being net sellers of silver into the market from 1990 through 2005, to being net buyers of silver in 2006. The last time this happened was 1979. . . . Prices rose from around $5.90 at the start of 1979 to a peak of $50 the following January.

But there are huge differences between 1980 and today. I'm convinced this silver bull will make the last one seem insignificant. For most of the 1980s, the public did what they always do. When they should have been investing in stocks, they chased yesterday's news and continued buying gold and silver. But that changed as we entered the 1990s. Investors who had paid $5 to $50 per ounce were caught up in the stock market craze that had started in the 1980s, and they sold their silver, usually at a loss, to purchase stocks. From 1990 to 2005 investors sold more silver than they bought . . . a lot more. Conversely, they bought a lot more stocks than they sold . . . a lot more.

According to the CPM Group, investors sold 1,654 million ounces of silver from 1990 to 2005. That's almost nine times the amount investors sold in the 1970s.

And it's not only the public that has been shedding their silver holdings. Governments around the world have stopped using silver as coinage and have been selling off their stockpiles. Look at Chart 26.

In fact, since the 1960s, a time when every government on the planet had significant silver reserves and used silver as coinage, and a time when the U.S. controlled 3.5 billion ounces (the single largest silver stockpile in history), all governments have been selling off their silver inventories. This extra supply has had the effect of artificially depressing the price. Today governments

Chart 26. Government Silver Inventories

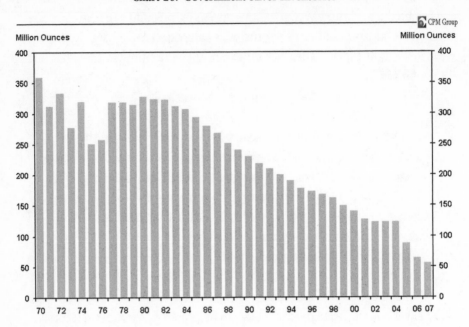

around the world are effectively out of silver. These government fire sales were accompanied by investor sales of around 1.6 billion ounces from 1990 to 2005. This had the effect of artificially depressing silver's price to such low levels that in many cases the price was below mining costs, putting some primary silver producers out of business.

Industrial Grade

So you might be asking yourself, *If the government was selling silver, and investors were selling silver, just who was buying silver?* The answer: industrial manufacturers. The silver that was sold was used to make consumer goods.

Of all the elements, silver is *the* indispensable metal. It is the most electrically conductive, thermally conductive, and reflective. Modern life, as we know it, would not exist without silver. Photography, batteries, electronics . . . these things all came of age, and became widely available, during, or shortly after, World War II, and then absolutely exploded in use after the 1960s due to scientific discoveries regarding the industrial applications of silver. Unlike silver, gold only has two basic uses, and both are hoarding type uses where the metal doesn't get used up . . . money and jewelry. Less than 10 percent of gold production is used in industrial applications. Ninety percent of all the gold ever mined throughout history is still available for purchase somewhere.

Silver, on the other hand, has hundreds of industrial uses and applications. Here is but a small example of the multitude of uses for silver: batteries, bearings, biocides, brazing, catalysts, coins, electrical conductors, electronics, electroplating, jewelry, medical applications, mirrors and reflective coatings, photography, silverware, solar energy cells, soldering, water purification.

Of all the uses for silver, only jewelry and silverware result in saving the silver used; in all other uses, silver gets used up in microscopic amounts, thrown away, and eventually ends up in a landfill. That's where those billions of ounces went!

In 1980 there were 2.5 billion ounces of silver that investors could buy, and by 1990 it stood at 2.1 billion ounces. Today, stockpiles are almost nonexistent. The point is that for the first time in history, of the available quantities that investors can buy, silver is more rare than gold.

Of the once mighty silver stockpile the United States held in the late 1950s and early 1960s, only 0.0056 percent remains. It has dwindled from 3.5 *billion* ounces to a mere 20 *million* ounces. And the rest of the world's governments have followed suit. We have gone from a world in which every country used silver as money, and also held large stockpiles of silver in reserve, to a world that is just about out of silver. In fact, if you add up all government stockpiles of silver worldwide, the total is only 0.016 percent of what just the United States *alone* used to hold. As longtime silver expert David Morgan of Silver-Investor.com puts it, "Gold is still held by many governments . . . silver is held by virtually none."

Chart 27, from the CPM Group, shows the total known world stockpiles of gold (light column) and silver (dark column), in 1990, and 2007. As you can see, there is *almost no silver left!*

Note that stockpiles of gold are growing, while silver stockpiles have shrunk dramatically. In 1979, when investors became net buyers of silver, driving silver to over $52 in 1980, there were more than 2.5 billion ounces of silver available for them to buy. Today, just as investors have once again become net buyers, silver inventories have almost vanished. And if you took

Chart 27. Precious Metals Bullion Stocks

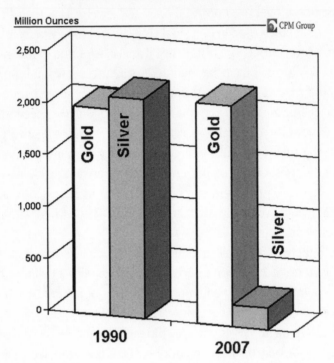

Economics 101, then you know what happens when demand increases and supply decreases.

Chart 28 depicts this drawdown of stocks of silver, but it measures it in a different and far more important way: in how many months the stocks of silver would last, at whatever the rate of consumption is at any given time, if worldwide mine production stopped. So the chart is basically an inventory/usage ratio, measured in how much time is left until all the silver is gone.

At the current rate of usage, the amount of time that aboveground stocks of silver would last if all mining activity were to cease is now down to just four months.

One thing that can be learned from Chart 28 is that once the inventory/usage ratio has bottomed, it is flashing a buy signal, and, unlike previous cycles, it isn't possible for this ratio to go any lower than it is. In fact, it's

Chart 28. Silver Bullion Inventories as Months of Demand

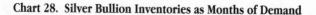

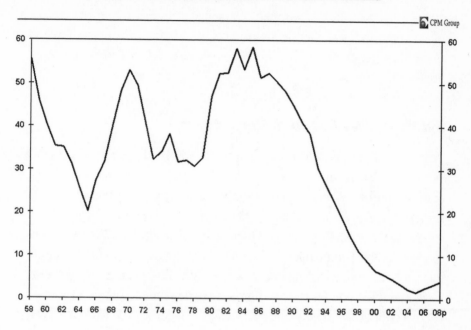

so absurdly low that it's unbelievable the public hasn't already realized how massively undervalued silver is, and it's absolutely astounding that bazillions of dollars haven't already flowed toward silver.

No, I take that back. It's not unbelievable at all. The public always chases yesterday's news. When they're busy investing in tulips or tech stocks, it sucks currency away from other sectors, and many things become incredibly undervalued. This happens to be silver's time to shine. I often say, "Gold is as cheap as dirt right now, but silver's cheaper than dirt."

Stinking Thinking

The only reason silver is so cheap right now is because people "think" it should be cheap. They've been conditioned to think that because governments have been dumping their silver into the markets for half a century. This extra supply has had the effect of suppressing silver's price, and the low price has resulted in our consuming more silver than we produced for over half a century. And as of 2007 governments pretty much have run out of silver, and they've stopped selling just as investor interest is rising. But as you now know, there is almost no silver left for investors to buy. And again, Economics 101: When there is great demand and minimal supply, prices will skyrocket.

But Won't They Just Mine More Silver?

That's a good question. The short answer is: yes. But the good news for silver investors is that most silver supplies don't come from silver mining operations. Rather, silver supplies are often a by-product of mining copper, lead, zinc, and gold. In fact, about 75 percent of the supply of newly mined silver originates as a by-product of mining other metals. This silver is a bonus to these mining companies and, as David Morgan points out, "A copper miner certainly is not going to throw the silver out." So, they sell it on the market; but the point is their business is not dependent on the price of silver. If a copper miner gets one percent of his income from silver, he's certainly not going to dig up ten times more copper to increase his silver production by a factor of ten.

So, the burden to satisfy silver demand falls on the shoulders of what are known as primary silver producers, and they're a rare breed. Currently silver mine production stands at a little over 500 million ounces per year. Primary silver producers only produce 25 percent of that, or 125 million ounces per year. If you could freeze demand where it is today, and the primary silver producers were able to double production, it would take more than fifteen years to get silver inventories back to the level they were in 1990.

But Won't They Just Open More Silver Mines?

Good question again. And again the short answer is yes. But the worldwide average for taking a mine from discovery to production is five to seven years, and in countries with strong environmental laws, it can take much longer. In the United States, for instance, even if you found a deposit of pure silver or gold, if it were in a state like California, you wouldn't ever get a permit to mine it due to the state's stringent environmental laws. Additionally, the big prospecting won't start until the price is at much higher levels. And to top it all off, due to the long bear market in precious metals there is a severe shortage of experienced workers with the specialized knowledge required for mining operations.

The world isn't just running out of silver aboveground either, it's also running out of silver *in* the ground. Minable deposits of silver are becoming harder to find. Ray De Motte, president of Sterling Mining, recently told me that the ratio of minable silver to gold might be less than 8 to 1 today, versus 12 to 1, or greater, in the past.

And the United States Geological Survey (USGS) concurs. Izzy Friedman, mentor to famed silver expert Theodore Butler, discovered an amazing fact buried in the USGS annual mineral reports. At current rates of production, there is less minable silver left in the earth's crust than any other metal.

According to the USGS, at current rates of production, the two metals we will run out of first are gold and silver. At these rates gold reserves will be exhausted in thirty years, and silver in just twenty-five.

The Coming Silver Boom

Given the dire economic circumstances we've been talking about in this book, you already know that the U.S. currency is doomed. And if I've done my job, you're also convinced that the next big transfer of wealth will come from precious metals and commodities. I'm certain that one of the biggest catalysts for growth in precious metals will come from silver. Indeed, I think we are on the verge of the greatest silver boom history has ever seen.

As the dollar continues to collapse, big investors will first turn toward gold and dramatically drive up its price. By the time the public catches on, gold will look pretty expensive to them. Everybody will then start hearing about silver being rarer than gold. In a frenzy, people will dive into silver, just as the stockpiles are practically diminished and production has practically stopped. That is when silver prices will explode.

The Fuses

There are four fuses that will ignite silver's prices:

FUSE #1: PRICE MANIPULATION

As we've already covered, the price of silver is manipulated, and it is manipulated to an even greater extent than the price of gold.

Ted Butler has been writing about this for many years. To my knowledge, Butler was the very first person to write about the price manipulation of gold and silver, and for ten years he has been waging a one-man war against price manipulations. It seems that certain entities have been using the New York Commodities and Mercantile Exchange (COMEX) to manipulate the silver price by unloading a lot, and I mean *a lot*, of silver onto the market. The big problem is that the silver that is being sold doesn't exist. It's bought and sold in futures contracts, papers that promise to deliver silver someday down the road.

How much is a lot, you might ask? Well, commodities traders on the COMEX have made bets in which they have promised to deliver more than double all the silver known to exist. If the longs (the traders who bought these futures contracts) demanded delivery from the shorts (the traders who sold these contracts), the rest of the world would have to go without silver for more than a year. That means no new cell phones or computers, Sonys or Panasonics, for more than a year.

There is no other commodity that has such a large short position. For instance, the amount of gold sold in futures contracts amounts to only 2.5 percent of known inventory. By contrast, the amount of silver sold in futures contracts amounts to more than 200 percent of all known inventory. That's a short position that is eighty times greater than gold's.

Is that alone proof that the price of silver is manipulated? No, but it's mighty suspicious. Something even more suspicious is the fact that silver also has the largest percentage of contracts (it's called open interest), held by the fewest number of traders, of any commodity. Only four traders hold the vast majority of silver short positions, and Ted Butler speculates that just one or two of them may hold more than 50 percent of all short positions. That would mean that just one or two entities are largely determining the price of silver for the

Chart 29. Days of Production to Cover the Short Positions of the 4 Largest Traders

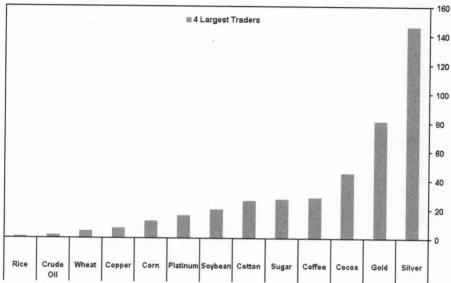

Source: World Gold Charts @ www.sharelynx.com

rest of the world. Just look at Chart 29. These four traders have sold, for future delivery, more than four months' worth of worldwide silver production.

Here is the good news. Since this artificial paper silver market dwarfs the physical silver market, the paper market is setting the price of silver. All this paper silver that has been sold has depressed the price of silver even further. In other words, silver is a lot cheaper than it should be, and that means you can buy it cheap—but not for long.

There will come a day when most of our physical silver holdings are gone, and no matter how much paper silver is sold into the market, physical silver will once again begin to set the price as short sellers are unable to deliver on their contracts and silver shortages develop. Then watch out, the shorts will be caught in a short squeeze that will ignite silver prices.

FUSE #2: LEASED SILVER
One fairly common practice you've probably never heard of is silver leasing. Silver leasing takes place when a silver producer has customers who want to

buy silver, but that producer has no silver on hand to sell. What does he do? He borrows (leases) the silver from someone who has a big pile of the stuff (like the central banks used to have), and promises to return the silver someday in the future. The producer then sells the silver to his buyer.

The problem with silver leasing (and gold leasing for that matter) is that the loans are never really paid back. Instead, they are rolled over into more loans. By some estimates, in order for all gold and silver leases to be repaid, mining production would have to be 100 percent devoted to the task for two years. That means no jewelry, cell phones, laptops, etc. would be produced during that time.

All of these leases create a phantom supply. As Theodore Butler has pointed out in his article "Silver Leasing or Silver Fleecing?," there are 150 million ounces of gold and one billion ounces of silver on loan in today's markets, of which there are currently no reserve supplies to use for payback. So, what does this phantom supply do? It suppresses pricing. Eventually the whole precious metals leasing system will collapse, and when it does, this phantom supply will disappear and pricing will go through the roof.

FUSE #3: SILVER CERTIFICATES

I'll be covering silver certificates in far greater detail later in the book, but it is important to touch on them here.

I talked with Ted Butler a couple of times before writing this. When I came to the subject of companies that offer silver certificates, he talked about trusted financial firms that provide storage for customers to whom they have sold silver. The problem is they are selling imaginary silver. He explained that when he first began writing about the phantom silver supply, people thought he was crazy. But then, on October 23, 2007, he posted an article titled "Money for Nothing." The gist of his article was that Morgan Stanley was sued for not actually storing precious metals, such as silver, even though it was charging clients for storage fees. The worst part is it didn't even refute the claim. Rather, it said it had done nothing wrong "by charging storage on metal that didn't exist, as this is a widespread industry practice."

Ted Butler's phrase for this practice is "un-backed silver storage accounts." Essentially, big firms like Morgan Stanley get to hold on to your cash and use it interest free for as long as you hold on to your silver account—which is generally a very long time for most investors. During that period of time, they are not obligated to actually have any silver on hand to back your currency. Even worse, some firms, like Morgan Stanley, still charge you storage fees for the silver that doesn't even exist. Basically, just as with precious metals leases, this is one big fraud. When, not if, a run on silver happens in the future, these institutions won't have the reserves on hand to pay up. This will leave people with physical silver reserves sitting very pretty as prices blow up thanks to the short fuse of silver shorts.

FUSE #4: EXCHANGE-TRADED FUNDS (ETFS)

Many of my colleagues in the precious metals industry believe the ETFs—exchange-traded funds—may not have all of the metals they say they do, and may be another tool for manipulating the price of gold and silver.

This may or may not prove to be true. If it is true, and they're playing the same hanky-panky as Morgan Stanley, then the price of the metals will go ballistic when the manipulation is exposed. If it isn't true, and the ETFs are 100 percent legitimate, then it's an even bigger fuse. Because of their explosive growth, they devour enormous quantities of gold and silver.

If you are going to *trade* gold and/or silver, instead of investing in gold and/or silver, then I wholeheartedly endorse and recommend the ETFs. They have, by far, the narrowest bid/ask spread (the difference between the price you pay when you buy, and what you get when you sell), highest liquidity, and can be bought and sold just like a stock on any trading platform. But, if you are *investing* in gold and silver for the long haul, then I urge you to investigate them carefully before you select them as your investment vehicle.

The Detonators

Now that we've established the fuses for the silver boom, let's talk about the detonators. The detonators are a series of likely events that will ignite the fuses we've just talked about. They are:

STOCKPILING

David Morgan of Silver-Investor.com says that when "commercial users sense a coming shortage . . . silver will show price strength that few believe possible at this point. Why? Because, at that point, silver users in the defense, automobile and electronics industries will all be competing for silver at the same time that investors will sense the profit potential." What that means is that industrial buyers will begin to buy as much silver as possible in order to stockpile it for use in the production of their goods. This will significantly reduce the supply in the market and cause prices to rise.

LARGE BUYERS

Sometime, someone, somewhere, will try to take a very large position in silver. Bill Gates probably carries enough cash in his wallet to buy all the silver in the world at today's prices.

MUTUAL FUNDS

For decades, brokerage houses used to recommend putting at least 10 percent of your net worth into gold, as a hedge against economic instability. Today, Wall Street has forgotten that golden rule, and 99 percent of investors don't have any precious metals in their portfolio. As the problems in the economy, banking sector, and Wall Street start to become clear to more investors, and as mutual funds look to the gains precious metals have made, many funds will add precious metals to their mix, and many of those will see silver's potential for superior gains.

FUTURE MEDIA

As you will see later in the book, gold and silver will become an economic bubble someday, just as stocks and real estate are today. When they do, gold and silver will be front-page news and the awareness of silver's rarity will go from something one in every 100,000 people know about, to something everybody knows about.

THE PUBLIC PERCEPTION

When the general public finally awakens from its coma and comes charging in, it will correctly reason that $50 silver can more easily double than can $2,000 gold. As Ted Butler says, "People don't like silver because you get too much for your money." The point being that often people think that the cheaper something is in terms of dollars, the less value it has. That is not always the case, and that perception, at least when it comes to silver, will change . . . just as it did in 1979.

And here's the best part. Any one of these detonators could cause the supply of physical silver to become nearly nonexistent. When that happens, all those precious metals leases and phantom supplies will ignite a silver explosion bigger than ever imaginable.

The Silver Safety Net

One last great thing about silver as an investment is it has a built-in safety net, at least at today's low prices. Since I've been buying silver, I've watched the price climb from $4.25 to $21. I've also invested in many of the mining companies, and the whole time I've watched silver climb and the stock prices soar, most of the mining companies still don't show a profit.

This is important to understand because in a world that is running out of silver, one of the most sought after industrial metals, it is impossible to sustain pricing that is below the cost of production for the majority of producers. The price cannot go down and stay down. It must eventually rise significantly above the cost of production in order to encourage enough prospecting and new mining to meet demand.

The best part about this safety net is that it has been getting even safer as the price of silver goes up. The majority of the costs associated with mining are related to the cost of energy. As silver has risen, so has the cost of oil. If you think oil will continue to rise in the future . . . then your safety net will only grow safer.

Back to the Future

So where do I think that silver's price will go? That's not really important. As I've said before, "The price means nothing! What's the value?"

I can honestly say that silver is extremely undervalued at the present time, which brings us right back to the beginning of this chapter. Remember that for the first 2,000 years of history the exchange rate between gold and silver was 12 ounces of silver to 1 ounce of gold on average.

Now here's the exciting part. Given enough time, values always revert to the mean. But when something is severely out of whack, it will usually overshoot the mean before settling back in. The longer and further out of whack it is, the further it will usually overshoot.

For more than a century, the gold/silver ratio has been further out of whack than anything I have ever heard of, and as I write this, the exchange rate between silver and gold is over 50 to 1. You can bet that when a run on silver happens, this ratio will come screaming back, and I'm pretty confident that it will snap way past the historical average of 12 to 1. And, because there is less silver than gold for investors to buy, I believe it may even go so far as to meet or exceed the price of gold. Now you know why silver really is a *precious* metal.

Part 3

Tomorrow

Chapter 12

The Pendulum

Throughout this book I have been talking about cycles, and the effects they have on the markets, the economy, and your investments. If you study long enough, I believe you'll come to the conclusion that just about everything happens in waves and cycles.

Cycles are everywhere in nature, but as a product of human nature, financial and commodity markets also exhibit cyclical behavioral patterns. These periods of optimism and pessimism seem to rise and fall with predictable regularity. But the length of different cycles can span days, weeks, months, years, decades, and even centuries. Thus, planning for such events is difficult due to the absence of previous experience with such cycles.

This is one of the reasons that financial education is so important, and why I'm proud to work with someone like Robert Kiyosaki, who believes that financial education and financial intelligence are key to surviving in today's economy. You can read more about Robert's commitment to financial education in his book *Rich Dad's Increase Your Financial IQ*, one of the best books on the importance of financial intelligence I've ever read.

As proof that these cycles are real, and of the enormous effect they can have on your wealth strategy, I want to briefly cover some common cycles.

The Stock Valuation Cycle, or the Price to Earnings Ratio Cycle

Over long periods of time the markets tend to run hot and cold. For simplicity's sake, I'm going to say that the price to earnings ratio (P/E ratio) is simply a measurement of how overvalued or undervalued a stock is. When stocks are experiencing a vigorous bull market, the market gets hot, everybody wants in, prices are high, and stocks become overvalued resulting in a high P/E. In a bear market, the market turns cold, everyone wants out, prices fall, and stocks become undervalued resulting in a low P/E.

The Tangible to Intangible Assets Cycle, or the Paper to Hard Assets Cycle

There is a cycle that measures the public's preference for intangible assets, meaning paper assets such as stocks, or tangible assets such as gold, real estate, commodities, or collectibles. There is no better example of this than the Dow/gold ratio. It is simply the points of the Dow, divided by the price of gold. The result is the value of the Dow measured in gold, or how many ounces of gold one share of the Dow costs.

Real Estate Cycle

If you price real estate in terms of ounces of gold instead of dollars you'll discover that just like the stock market, real estate follows the same cycle, from overvalued, to undervalued, and back again.

Chart 30 shows the P/E ratio of the Dow, the Dow's value measured in gold, and the value of real estate, also measured in gold, from the year 1920 to the present. You can clearly see them swinging back and forth in cycles that are quite evident. Also note that the timing of the cycles for all three items, P/E, Dow/gold, and real estate/gold, are almost identical.

From the 1929 stock market crash into the Great Depression, the P/E ratio, Dow/gold, and real estate/gold ratios fall at almost exactly the same time. Then real estate rebounds earlier than stocks, as thousands of soldiers come home from World War II, get married, buy a house, and start making the baby boom.

Chart 30. Homes Priced in Gold, P/E Ratio, Dow Priced in Gold

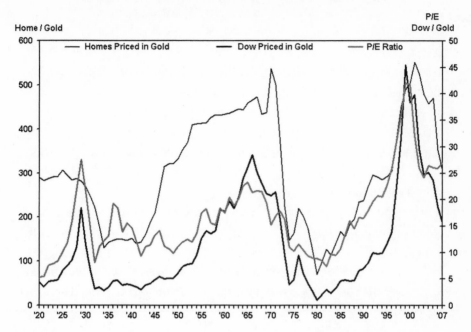

Source: Robert J. Shiller, Professor of Economics, Yale University; National Association of Realtors

Then note that, once again, stocks and real estate fall in value simultaneously compared to gold. This was not stocks and real estate falling, as much as it was gold rising in value as it did its accounting of all of the dollars that had been created since 1934. But proof that it is part of the cycle is in the fact that P/E ratio went along for the ride. Then you can see the greatest stock market boom in history begins in 1980 and, simultaneously, gold began a grueling twenty-year bear market.

But then at the turn of this century, something truly astounding is revealed. Since the year 2000, the great rebound of the stock markets and the greatest real estate boom in history have been nothing but mirages. The whole time they have been going up in price, they have been falling in value. And it isn't just because gold has been rising faster than stocks and real estate. The falling P/E ratio confirms that something more fundamental is taking place.

My business associate, Brent Harmes, has been studying cycles for many years now, and has become quite an expert. Cycles are his professional passion. He studies as many investment cycles as he can dig up and has identified several key cycles that are critical for investor success. He believes that investors who look at how history has repeated, instead of listening to what the crowd says, will be proven correct every time.

As Brent points out, "The pendulum doesn't stop halfway. It has to overcorrect for the past excesses to be wrung out. In all the investments that had extreme overvalue we should expect extreme undervalue before a true bottom occurs. In each of these cycles, the cycle is not over until the pendulum swings all the way to the other extreme."

Chart 30, which covers more than a century, is merely snapshot close-ups of a much larger picture. The three waves in each of the charts are just the most recent in a series of waves and cycles that go back to the beginnings of free market capitalism. There have been five of these waves in the United States over the past 200 years, and we are just beginning the sixth. It's called the commodity cycle.

Swimming with the Tide

Robert Kiyosaki often talks about controlling risk in your investment strategy. With such conclusive, absolute, indisputable proof, based on such a vast array of historical evidence, my conclusion is that betting against these tidal forces of investment cycles is placing your capital at great risk, while betting with them is practically no bet at all. In fact, I would say that investing with the financial currents can make even the uneducated investor look like a genius. Just look at how smart all the real estate flippers looked until the real estate bubble burst. But investors who do their due diligence, study the cycle they are in, and figure out ways to determine when a cycle is coming to an end, can simultaneously increase their potential gains while limiting their risk.

Let me show you just how powerful swimming with the tide can be. To do this, I'm going to once again use the Dow as a representation for blue-chip stocks. Now I'd like to tell you of two investors from long ago, Bob and Paul. Let's see how they do with two of the most conservative investments that currency can buy . . . gold and the Dow.

Both were born in 1903, and both became investors that same year when their parents bought them each one share of the Dow. The Dow bottomed out that year at a low of just 30 points. For luck, their parents had each used a $20 and $10 gold piece (1.5 ounces of gold).

By 1923 their conservative investment had tripled in price over the preceding twenty years, but then the stock market really took off and by 1929 each share was worth more than twelve times what their parents had paid. The year before, Bob met a beautiful blonde named Betty, and Paul met a plump little petunia named Patty, and both couples were married. Then in the summer of 1929, Bob and his blond bride, Betty, were blessed with a beautiful bouncing baby boy named Bubba, while Paul and Patty produced a pretty little princess named Pamela.

Bob had been saving for a new car and was just $100 shy from the $495 it would take to buy a brand-new Ford. But Bob was gripped in the euphoria of the stock market, so, in the tradition of his father and as a birthday gift to his new son, he took 18 ounces of gold ($380) and bought one share of the Dow at 380 points. But Paul was getting an uneasy feeling, figuring the market can't go up at this rate forever. So, in the summer of 1929, he cashed out, receiving 18 ounces of gold, which he held in trust for Pam.

Just a couple of months later the Dow crashed, and three years after that it bottomed at just 40 points (2 ounces of gold). Paul took the 18 ounces of gold he got from cashing out of the Dow in 1929, and bought nine shares of the Dow for his daughter, Pam. Pam's investment did very well over the next three decades, but in 1966 her father, Paul, now sixty-three and retired, telephoned her and shared a little secret with her. For many years he had been thinking about how lucky he had been to have an innate sense of when stocks had been overvalued or undervalued. It had fascinated him so much that he had been studying stock market valuations since he retired. He had stumbled upon a great secret: Valuations seem to swing back and forth like a great pendulum. He went on to explain to her what P/E ratios were, and how stocks were extremely overvalued at the time. He also had calculated that, measured in terms of gold, the Dow was one and a half times more overvalued than it was at the peak at which he had sold in 1929. Pam hung up the phone, called her broker, and sold her nine shares of the Dow. The next day she bought gold, and was delighted to find she got 252 ounces with the proceeds.

In the late '70s gold began to rocket and in January of 1980 gold was on the front page of the newspaper every day. Pam's father called again to tell her that, like the long lines in front of the coin shops, this mania people were feeling couldn't last. It reminded him of how the frenzy was in 1929. He also said that P/Es were at the lowest that they had been since 1932, and that stocks were extremely undervalued. The very next day gold hit $850; Pamela called her broker and told him to sell her gold and buy the Dow with the proceeds. Later that day, her broker called her back, and the news he had to give her absolutely amazed the both of them. Gold had hit $850, and the Dow was at 850 points on the same day, so her 252 ounces of gold bought her 252 shares of the Dow.

Paul died in 1990. He was eighty-seven. Pam thought of her father, and the lessons he had taught her, often. In 1999, when her gardener told her that she should invest in dot.com and tech stocks, she got an uneasy feeling. So this is what my father must have felt, she thought. She looked up the P/E of the Dow and found that it was 30 percent higher than the stock market peak before the crash of 1929. Next she divided the points of the Dow by the price of gold and found that, in terms of gold, stocks were almost two and a half times more overvalued than they were before the crash. She went to her computer, logged on to her brokerage account, and sold the Dow. A few days later she took the proceeds and bought 11,088 ounces of gold.

In March of 2008, Pam got a call from an old family friend, Bubba. Bubba's father, Bob, had died. He had lived to the incredible age of 105. Bubba shared that long ago Bob had passed along to him some financial wisdom that he had taken to heart, "live below your means, get out of debt, save money, and invest for the long term." He also shared how well he had done. He bragged that his share of the Dow that his father had bought him in 1929 was now worth $12,000, and that his father had left his sister a share that his grandfather had only paid $30 for in 1903. Pam didn't say anything. She already knew what her grandfather's $30 investment was worth, because the math was easy. She had 11,088 ounces of gold, and gold had just hit $1,000 per ounce. She was worth over $11 million. She realized there had been a long silence on the phone and she said, "$12,000 . . . that's great Bubba."

After the phone call Pam did some math. When she calculated Bubba's gains, the share his grandfather had bought for $30 had gained 39,900 percent in price and the share his father had paid $380 for had a price gain of 3,058 percent. But it was when she assessed the value in terms of gold that she could see things clearly. Bob had paid 18 ounces of gold for that one share of the Dow he bought for Bubba in 1929, but now that one share was only worth 12 ounces. Bubba had been invested in the Dow for his entire life, and, after seventy-nine years, the Dow had lost 33 percent of its value.

Pam already knew that the 1.5 ounces of gold her grandfather had invested had turned into 11,088 ounces. But it was when she did the math that she finally understood the immense power of the knowledge her father had passed down to her. The increase from 1.5 to 11,088 ounces of gold was a 739,100 percent gain in absolute value. But she was absolutely flabbergasted to find that, because of her father's instincts, and later the wisdom he had gained from studying the past, her grandfather's $30 investment had returned price gains of almost 37 million percent.

That was a fun story, but here is the best part. You don't have to wait 100 years for massive wealth to be transferred toward you. History shows that the greatest wealth is created in the shortest period of time, during the portion of the cycle where commodities are outperforming paper assets, and when the precious metals are revaluing themselves. In this example, the first time Paul and his descendants were invested in stocks they had to wait twenty-six years before the peak of the cycle; the second time it took thirty-four years; and the third time was twenty years. But, the time invested in gold was just three years the first time, fourteen years the second time, and currently it is at eight years and counting.

Generally, the Dow is undervalued in terms of gold when it costs less than 4 ounces of gold, valued fairly at about 6 or 7 ounces of gold, and overvalued when it costs more than 10 ounces of gold. But as we talked about in the last chapter, when something's way out of whack to one side, it usually overcorrects itself before it reverts to the mean (and everything always reverts to the mean). In 1929, the Dow was overvalued at 18 ounces, and when it reverted to the mean the pendulum overshot to 2 ounces. In 1966 the ratio was extremely overvalued at 28 ounces of gold per share, and in 1980 the pendulum overcorrected to a ratio of just 1 ounce per share.

Given today's economic conditions, I'm confident that the Dow/gold ratio will at least overshoot to 2, but it wouldn't surprise me in the least to see the Dow come off of its way, way, way overvalued peak in 1999 of 44 ounces of gold per share and overshoot to just one half ounce of gold per share or less. Right now the Dow/gold ratio is at 14, so that means that every ounce of gold I have today will probably buy me twenty-eight times more blue-chip stocks someday in the future.

There are, of course, many more examples of economic cycles I could give you, but suffice it to say, cycles exist, and an awareness of their existence and knowledge of how they work will greatly aid you in maximizing your investments.

As I said at the beginning of this book, "These cycles that ebb and flow throughout history are as natural as the coming of the tides. And while betting against them may be hazardous to your financial health, investing with them can bring you great wealth."

So I say you should swim with the tide, and right now the tide is flowing in the direction of commodities, especially gold and silver. Continue to educate yourself, study, play the Rich Dad *Cashflow* game, and read the rest of the Rich Dad books. Knowledge is power. Empower yourself and get ready to catch the next big wave. Because the only thing that stays the same is change.

Chapter 13

Golden Castles

Gold and Silver Versus Real Estate

Believe it or not, I firmly believe that passive income entities, like real estate, are the ultimate investment. Gold and silver are just the means I have chosen to get there. Even though I haven't mentioned it until now, my ultimate goal is to accumulate real estate, not gold and silver. Gold and silver do not cash-flow and there are no tax advantages. However, I firmly believe that, because of the cycle we are in, I can accumulate far more real estate by buying gold and silver now, than if I buy real estate now.

To illustrate this concept, let's look at the relationship between the housing and silver markets during the last big precious metals bull market.

The House That Silver Built

The S&P/Case-Shiller Home Price Index (S&P/CSI) says that in 1971, when the last great precious metals bull began, a median-price, single-family home in the United States was $20,663. The same year silver's average price was $1.39 per ounce. Thus, it required 14,823 ounces of silver to buy a median-price, single-family home in the U.S.

At the end of the precious metals bull in January 1980, just nine years later, that same home cost $42,747, and silver was just over $52.50 per ounce, so it required roughly 814 ounces of silver to buy the same home. The house had increased in price 2 times, or 100 percent. However, the currency supply had grown 2.45 times, or 145 percent. Inflation raged all through the 1970s, and the result was that though real estate increased significantly in price, its true value barely kept up with inflation and may have actually fallen a little. Conversely, silver had increased 3,641 percent, outpacing inflation by more than fifteen times.

Now, here's a really cool scenario. If you had sold a house in 1971 for $20,663 and purchased silver, by January 1980 your investment would have outpaced real estate by a factor of 17, growing to $770,796. If you then sold your silver, you could buy eighteen median-price, single-family homes, all cash, at the 1980 price of $42,747 per house and benefit from 100 percent of the cash flows from those properties, or, if you were feeling really adventurous, you could put 20 percent down and buy ninety homes for the same price.

Today, we find ourselves in a similar situation, only better. Real estate has become much more overvalued and silver has become extremely undervalued. Measured against silver, the median price, single-family home in the U.S. hit its peak in 2002, at a price of 38,123 ounces of silver, some two and a half times higher than at the beginning of the last precious metals bull market in 1971.

When silver hit its peak of $52.50 in 1980, it was not rare. Today, as we've already discussed in detail, identifiable aboveground silver stockpiles have been drawn down to a tiny fraction of their size in 1980.

When the gold and silver bull market explodes, the financial news will react just as it did in 1980, and the only thing you will hear about is gold and silver. At that time there will be market analysts all over the Internet, radio, and TV, proclaiming to everyone the greatest investment of all time—gold and silver! The rarity of silver will go from something that a small fraction of the world's population knows about to something everyone is now an expert on.

After studying things like the tulip mania of 1637, the Nasdaq bubble of the 1990s, the history and the current fundamentals of gold and silver, and the history of financial cycles, it would not surprise me in the least to see less than 500 ounces of silver buy a median-price, single-family home sometime in the future.

As of this writing, 500 ounces of silver is selling for around $9,000 (I would venture to bet that as you're reading this, it is selling for even more), and a median price, single-family home is selling for $200,000 (and I'll wager the home is selling for less as you read this). Wouldn't you love to buy a home outright, for just $9,000? Or put 20 percent down and buy five homes? Well, I believe that if you buy silver now, and wait until silver is once again over-valued and real estate is once again undervalued, you will be able to do so. Remember, in 1980 it only took 814 ounces of silver to purchase one home, and silver wasn't rare then.

If indeed the day comes that you can buy a median-price, single-family home in the U.S. for just 500 ounces of silver, then that means that if you owned a home outright, sold it now, and bought silver, then, when silver peaks against real estate, bought similar homes in the same neighborhood (barring tax losses), you could buy twenty-three of them outright, or 115 of them at 20 percent down. I know these figures sound silly, but believe it or not, they are not improbable. It's just a repeat of the 1970s bull with a little twist.

What these numbers show is that by going with the flow (right now the flow is in the direction of precious metals), and always betting in the direction of true value, your winnings are not only quite large, or even huge, but they are nearly unbelievable.

Given our housing example, even if you ended up losing 50 percent of your earnings to taxes and other costs, you could still end up owning about twelve homes outright or sixty-four at 20 percent down, all for the price of one home in today's dollars.

The biggest mean reversion in history is knocking on our door. I can't stress this enough. The good news is that everything always reverts to the mean, and the bad news is that everything always reverts to the mean. Whether the news is good or bad will depend on if you are invested in the correct asset class for the cycle you are currently in. Investors who are aware of this will have wealth knocking on their doors, whereas investors who are caught unaware may end up with collection agents knocking on theirs.

Measured in silver, real estate peaked in 2002, at a price of 38,123 ounces of silver for a median-price, single-family home (Chart 31). Real estate has

Chart 31. Homes Priced in Silver

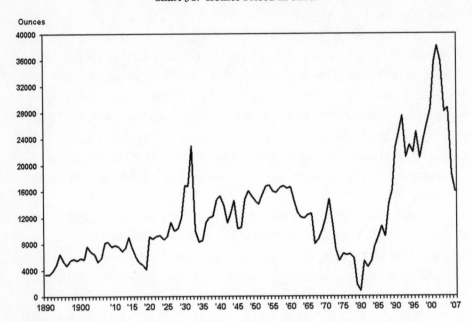

Source: Robert J. Shiller, Professor of Economics, Yale University, National Association of Realtors

never, *ever*, been this overvalued. And silver has never, ever, *ever*, been this undervalued.

The point of all this is that with real estate so overvalued, and silver so undervalued, chances are that they will both overshoot to the opposite extreme, before reverting to the mean. What that means for you is that you now have a very rare chance to become very wealthy very quickly by simply taking advantage of economic cycles and the wealth transfer they create.

Part 4

How to Invest in Precious Metals

Chapter 14

Beware the Pitfalls

Up to this point there has been a huge amount of information thrown at you. If you haven't ever studied the history of currencies, economic cycles, and all of the other topics we've covered in this book, it can be a lot to take in. But I assure you there is a method to my madness.

All of this history and theory we've been going over is good for one thing, and one thing only. Equipping you with the knowledge you'll need to invest wisely in real money . . . and, if the dollar survives, you might just make a bunch of currency while you're at it.

So, the rest of this book is devoted to giving you practical application on all the information we've covered. By the time we're done, I promise you will be confident and ready to invest in precious metals, and ready to take advantage of the immense wealth transfer that is coming our way.

And we're going to start by learning what *not* to do when investing in precious metals.

The Pits!

Way back in the day, when video games were just beginning to catch on, Atari put out their now famous video game console for home use. One of the games available to play was called *Pitfall!* The premise was simple. You played an adventurer exploring distant jungles in search of hidden treasures. This was not sophisticated stuff. It basically involved jumping over dangerous animals and swinging on vines over vast pits. If you didn't time your jumps right, you fell into the pits and had to start the level over again. Hence the title *Pitfall!* The game was deceptively simple, and too often a player would quit in frustration, having fallen into the same pit over and over again.

I was thinking about that game as I sat down to write this chapter, and it became apparent to me that after having read all the material we've covered so far in this book, investing in precious metals might also actually seem deceptively simple. The truth is that, just like the Atari game, there are many pitfalls that can waylay a precious metals investor. They may not be tar pits and cliffs, but they are just as real. And they usually come in the form of scams.

When I was initially talking with Robert Kiyosaki about writing this book for the Rich Dad series, he specifically asked for a chapter on all the scams, cons, and pitfalls associated with investing in precious metals. I wholeheartedly agreed.

But just as a newspaper headline usually makes things appear worse than they really are, the stories below make it look like the entire precious metals industry is populated with nothing but con artists and thieves. I assure you, that's not the case. The precious metals industry is full of good people who want to serve you well, hoping that you'll become a valued, repeat customer. It's the dangerous few, however, that you have to guard against. That's why knowing what not to do when investing in precious metals is just as important (if not more so) than knowing what to do.

Exchange-Traded Funds: (ETFs)

The acronym ETF stands for exchange-traded fund. It's a security that trades like a stock, but is supposed to track the price of an index like the Dow or S&P 500 instead of an individual company; or it may be designed to track the price of a commodity like oil, gold, or silver. The ETFs for gold and silver can be very good vehicles for *trading*. But they can also be a major pitfall for *investing*.

Many of my colleagues in the precious metals industry have come to distrust the ETFs, and view them with great suspicion. Some even feel that they are yet another tool for manipulating the price of gold and silver.

James Turk of GoldMoney has spent countless hours poring over the disclosure statements and Securities and Exchange Commission filings of gold and silver ETFs, and what he discovered is quite disturbing.

Regarding the silver ETF, iShares Silver Trust, the SEC filings say things like, "the liquidity of the iShares may decline and the price of the iShares may fluctuate independently of the price of silver and may fall" and "The iShares are intended to constitute a simple and cost-effective means of making an investment *similar* to an investment in silver."

I've got two questions. If the iShares are fully backed by physical silver, then how could they diverge from the price of silver and fall? And also, what does "an investment *similar* to an investment in silver" mean?

Again, I urge you to investigate these vehicles before buying them. Just do an Internet search for James Turk's articles: "Can We Trust the Silver ETF?" and "The Paper Game."

One of the main reasons for holding precious metals is that they are one of the few financial assets that you can hold outside the financial system. And as we have seen lately, the financial system isn't quite as sound as they'd like you to think. When you buy an ETF, you are buying shares in a trust that is owned and run by a bank, which might be holding gold or silver. But shares in an ETF are *not* gold or silver, which is allocated to, and wholly owned by, a single entity, YOU!

Pools and Certificates

Gold and silver "pool accounts" and "certificate programs" should really be called "IOU Gold or Silver Someday" accounts. In his article "Buyer Beware," Theodore Butler of Butler Research (ButlerResearch.com) warns, "These are purely paper promises or bookkeeping-only entries."

Why would anyone invest in one of these accounts? Simple. First, it's cheap and easy, and we all love cheap and easy, don't we? Second, Customers *think* they're buying gold or silver, but they're really buying a promise to deliver gold or silver someday. Here's a simple rule of thumb: If there are no storage fees, then most likely, there's nothing being stored.

More evidence that there is no real metal in these accounts is provided by the fact that if you ever want to take delivery of the gold or silver that you supposedly own, you must pay a "fabrication charge." Fabrication charge? Is this pool account some big ambiguous blob of metal, or perhaps a real pool of liquid metal that they have to fabricate a bar from? No, this is simply a charge to bring the bid/ask spread up to what it would have been had you purchased real gold or silver in the first place.

When looking at these types of investment vehicles, it's important to examine the bid/ask spread. The bid/ask spread is the difference between the price a dealer charges you when you buy, and what he'll pay you when you sell. I looked at the bid/ask spread of a well-known bullion dealer, and the spread was four to ten times higher on physical gold products than the spread on their pool account, and there are no storage fees. So how do they make their money? According to Ted Butler, they make it by using the buyer's money to fund their investment activities.

The big problem with pools and certificates is that the companies running them are basically short the metals; they take your currency but don't go out and buy real money (gold or silver), and store it for you. It is the same thing as selling gold or silver short. When the day comes that you want to cash out, the price may have risen significantly, and they either have to go out into the market and buy the metal at the going price, or cough up the difference in cash.

How is this accomplished? According to Butler, the issuer uses new investor cash to cover the spreads when an old investor wants out. The problem with this way of doing business is that once the price of gold or silver reaches a certain tipping point, more people will want to cash out than the issuer can cover. Then the whole thing implodes.

Leverage

Leverage can dramatically increase your winnings, and in the next chapter I will be recommending leverage for those who are educated in the proper techniques and are skilled in its use. But if you don't know what you're doing (and sometimes even if you do), using leverage to invest can result in devastating losses. It's this simple: When you introduce leverage, you introduce risk.

In the case of buying on margin, you are going up against a mathematical formula and compounding fees that are engineered to work against the novice. In the case of futures contracts, you are working against time because you've introduced an expiration date. In the case of options, you're adding the decay of the options value over time to the expiration date, and you are going up against an opponent in a winner-takes-all game, not dissimilar to a high-stakes game of poker or a duel at high noon against a gunslinger in the Old West.

Leverage is the realm for professionals who know the odds and the numbers, and they know how to eat the little guy for breakfast. You never know who's taking the other side of the bet in an options play. Many times you are going up against very deep pocket traders such as mutual funds and hedge funds. Either way, if you're not better than they are . . . you're in trouble.

Gold and Silver Purchased on Margin

Buying gold or silver on margin is a double-edged sword, but the two edges are not equally sharp. Because of the mathematics of margin, the edge that cuts against you is much sharper than the edge that cuts for you, and if you're not careful, it'll cut you deeply.

In a margined account, you can buy a whole lot more of the stock or commodity than your funds will allow. The way this works is sort of like buying a home. You put a little down, say 20 percent, and your broker will loan you the rest of the money for your purchase, using your 20 percent equity as collateral. Unlike a home, however, you don't have to make payments. Instead, if the investment rises in price, it automatically pays down the loan with the profits. The downside of this is that if your investment falls in price, instead of paying off the loan, the difference in price is now eating away at your equity. Once your equity falls below a certain percent, your broker forecloses, and you're out in the street.

Here is the way margin works against you. Let's say you put up $100 as your investment position. If the margin requirement set by your broker is 20 percent, then your broker will loan you the other 80 percent (in this case $400).

So now, with only a $100 investment you can control $500 worth of stock, and you are now leveraged at 5 to 1. If the stock goes up 10 percent to $550, your profit on your original $100 investment is $50, a 50 percent gain. Again, that's a leverage of 5 to 1. The stock went up 10 percent but your gains were 50 percent.

But now your broker applies the $50 profit against your loan, so now you own $150 worth of the $550 worth of stock that you control (27 percent equity). You are now only leveraged at 3.7 to 1. If the stock rises another 10 percent to $605 you have a profit of $55 and a gain of only 37 percent. Now your $55 profit raises your equity to $205, and you are now only leveraged at 2.95 to 1. The next time the stock goes up 10 percent your payoff is only going to be 29.5 percent. This process repeats itself until the stock has made enough profit to pay off your loan, at which point your leverage is zero.

So, the leverage working for you is sort of a blunt instrument, diminishing as your stock rises. But what about the downside, what happens when your stock falls?

Using the same scenario, if you had a $100 investment in a $500 stock position, and the price of your stock falls 10 percent, you have a $50 loss, or 50 percent (the same 5 to 1 leverage you had on the way up). But now the $50 is deducted from your equity of $100, leaving only $50 of equity on $450 worth of stock. You now have just a little more than 11 percent equity, and you are now leveraged at a whopping 9 to 1 ratio. If your stock drops a further 10 percent to $405, you lose $45, or 90 percent of your remaining equity. Long before you get to this point, however, you'll get a margin call and your broker will give you the opportunity to cough up the cash to bring your position up to the minimum margin requirement within twenty-four to forty-eight hours; if not, he'll liquidate your position (foreclose).

And don't forget the interest your broker will charge you for the loan. (You didn't think he was going to give it to you for free, did you?) This typically ranges between 1.3 to two times the rate of the best home loans currently being offered. In other words, it's fairly high interest.

Also, if you're using margin to leverage metals, to all of the above you must add the storage and brokerage fees. When you add the interest and storage fees together, the chances of making a profit become even slimmer. For instance, back in 2003–2004, when the Fed funds rate was just one percent, and home loans 5 percent, if you didn't show more than a 12 percent to 15 percent annual profit on your leveraged metals, you were underwater.

The point is that the double-edged sword of margin is about as sharp as a butter knife on the way up, but it cuts like a surgical laser on the way down.

Futures and Options

As I have said: Leverage is the realm of the professionals. If you are adept at its use, it can magnify your winnings tremendously; if you are unskilled, you *will* suffer the consequences. Futures and options are types of leverage. Futures are contracts to deliver a specific commodity, in an agreed quantity, at an agreed price, on an agreed date in the future. They are traded like stocks on numerous commodity exchanges around the world. So a futures contract is really nothing but an IOU.

Commodities are the tangible things that we eat, use, and/or buy. The commodities that are traded are things like cattle, cocoa, coffee, copper, corn, cotton, and crude oil. Gold, silver, and platinum are also traded on the commodity exchanges as futures contracts.

Futures contracts are highly leveraged trading vehicles, and options on futures are leveraged to the max. The elation from the payoffs can be enormous, but the pain from the losses can be excruciating.

If you want to experience the elation with far less accompanying pain, please get educated before using leverage. I'm sure there are many good programs out there, but the one I'm familiar with, and so the one I recommend, is Rich Dad's education courses on options trading. You can find out more at RichDad.com

When you invest in futures you must seriously consider whether or not you are playing the expert's game. As the great gold and silver rush of the twenty-first century progresses, those who make the rules will once again change the rules. In 1980, the COMEX (Commodities Exchange) and the CFTC (Commodity Futures Trading Commission) changed the rules to "liquidation orders only," and capped the price of silver. "Liquidation only" means that participants can only close out existing futures contracts. No new contracts could be created, so with no new buyers, the price can only go down.

There is an inevitable default coming on the commodities exchanges, especially with regard to silver. It is entirely possible that you could see the price of silver on the exchanges frozen, while the price of physical silver continues to rocket north.

This is called backwardation, which is when the price of a commodity costs more for delivery today than it does for delivery in the future. This happened to silver when one man, Warren Buffett, took delivery of 129.7 million ounces of silver from futures contracts in 1998. When he suddenly asked for delivery of his silver, instead of settling in cash, there was a scramble to find enough silver to fulfill his contracts. Not only did he single-handedly drive the price of silver from $4.25 to $7.75 in just six months, but, at the peak, caused a huge backwardation where silver for immediate delivery sold at a significant premium.

If there was a default on the commodities exchanges during the coming gold and silver rush, I believe you would see the exchanges change the rules to liquidation orders only, or even freeze the prices of all open contracts, while gold and silver prices for immediate delivery and "off exchange" silver (silver that is in private hands or in depositories that are not part of the commodities exchanges) continues to shoot to the moon. In this case, anybody who is playing their game, whether it is futures contracts, or through an entity that is just giving you exposure to the price of the metals (by itself possibly being exposed to futures), will be left out in the cold. I remind you of this clause from the silver ETF: "the liquidity of the iShares may decline and the price of the iShares may fluctuate independently of the price of silver and may fall."

There is a default coming in silver futures, where sellers of paper silver will not be able to get the physical silver to deliver. When that day comes they— the COMEX (Commodities Exchange), the CFTC (Commodity Futures Trading Commission), and the ETFs—*will* change the rules. How would you like it if you had a large position in silver and the big boys changed the rules so that the price of your silver was frozen, while the price of everyone else's silver continued its intergalactic trajectory? Don't play their game. Play your own game, by your own rules.

So, ETFs, pools, certificates, margin, futures, and options all share one thing in common: You're either going up against, or handing your currency over to, professionals.

As Eric Sprott, of Sprott Asset Management, reminds us, the financial establishment regards the small investor as "the plankton of the financial world." So, if you want to be the plankton of the financial world, go ahead and use leverage without an education. But, if you do, just know that it is quite likely that the they will slaughter you, carve you up, and dine on your financial carcass.

Numismatics

Numismatics is defined as the study or collecting of coins, medals, and paper money. Numismatic is the proper term for collector coins, and the word is derived from the Greek *numisma*, meaning "current coin."

When I am asked about numismatic coins as an investment I usually tell my customers that numismatic coins are beautiful, and in a bull market a few of them do very well. But the key words here are "a few." So if you want to invest in them, you'd better learn more about them than your dealer knows.

When I told this to one customer who called me, he said, "Yeah, I know. I bought $250,000 worth of supposedly rare numismatics a few years ago, and now that gold has doubled in price, I still can't find anyone that'll give me what I paid for these _____ things." (The missing word in that quote was not publishable, by the way.)

There are three layers of cost built into the price of a numismatic coin: metal content, numismatic premium, and dealer profit. Bullion and bullion coins, by contrast, have only two layers: metal content and dealer profit.

The numismatic premiums can vary from a few bucks to several million, depending on the coin. The most expensive coins, the rarest of the rare, will probably always be good investments because there are only a few of them. Only a few of the world's wealthiest collectors can own them. For the vast majority of collector coins, the numismatic premium is largely dependent on the state of the economy and the mood of the public. Dealer profits on numismatic coins can range from 15 percent to 100 percent (and in the case of the scams discussed later, 1,000 percent or more), whereas bullion, and bullion coins have no numismatic premium and typically command a dealer profit of only 1 percent to 5 percent.

A bullion coin's value is derived only from the worldwide spot price of the metal it's made from. Thus the potential number of buyers at any given moment can number in the millions, and the prices they are offering are all about the same. A numismatic coin's value, on the other hand, is derived from the yearning, passion, lust, desire, or covetousness of a particular buyer, and the price offered can vary wildly.

Before the era of computer-based trading and online auctions, finding the right buyer was largely a matter of sheer luck. But even today, at any given moment, the market for rare coins is very thin, and the value of your coin is dependent on whether you and that exact right buyer can find each other. There is a saying that goes something like this: "The only thing rarer than a rare coin . . . is a buyer for a rare coin."

That is unless you sell it back to your dealer. Dealers will always buy back your coins, but the profit that your dealer made on your numismatic coins to begin with was 15 percent to 100 percent. That means that the market price of your "investment" has to rise by 15 percent to 100 percent just for you to break even. On the other hand, if you're invested in bullion, and the price of gold or silver rises just 1 percent to 5 percent, you're in profit.

To be fair, since the inception in the mid-1980s of coin-grading services, the whole numismatic sector has come a long way. The coin-grading services have come close to standardizing the criteria that make coins special. They now inspect, grade, and encapsulate coins in a tamperproof clear-plastic container called a slab. The slab has an area on it that features a bar code, serial number, grade, and the rest of the coin's specifications. This has made the market much more liquid because you can now bid on a coin being auctioned online or through a dealer trading network, and you know what you're getting. But it's not perfect. The grading is reliant upon experts and is done by eye, and the opinions of the experts seem to vary significantly from grading service to grading service.

Also, some rare coins aren't as rare as people would like you to believe. The various coin-grading services have graded tens of millions of coins over the years, and now it has become popular to grade brand-new coins that have just been minted, like American Gold and Silver Eagles. Now a dealer can buy anything from a roll of pennies, to a sealed case of Gold Eagles from the U.S. Mint, send it to a coin-grading service where it will be removed from its container with gloved hands, inspected, graded, slabbed, and certified "Uncirculated." Now that it's bestowed with the magical powers that grading confers, that penny (which may have been minted by the billions) can now be sold for anywhere from $2 to $500, or even more. Again, it all comes down to demand and finding that mythical perfect buyer.

I think anyone buying "brand-new collectibles" is being taken for a ride. The whole reason that a 100-year-old, uncirculated coin is rare is because it was a complete accident. The coin was supposed to be circulated, but it got stuck in the back of a drawer somewhere, was part of a roll that somehow remained unopened, or (in the case of the U.S. Morgan Silver Dollar) the Treasury didn't release some of them until sixty to eighty years after they were minted.

A long time ago there was an article I read that had a quote that went something like this: "In numismatics, lots of money is made selling rare coins to noncollectors, and whenever a noncollector buys collector's items, the future loss of his capital is almost certainly guaranteed."

As you probably have surmised by now, I don't think much of numismatics as an investment. The reason is twofold. If you don't know what you're doing, you're probably going to lose, and, as I have said in previous chapters, I believe there is a currency crisis just waiting for us someday in the future.

Numismatics used to be known as the hobby of kings, but today everyone has gotten into the act. In the last great bull market some numismatic coins did spectacularly well. But in the 1970s, the middle class wasn't into coin collecting as they are today. In the midst of the currency crisis of the future, I'd expect that the numismatic premium on coins of questionable rarity could vanish as millions of collectors try to get liquid. When you're going to lose the car, or house, that yearning you had for those particular coins will take a back seat to survival.

Then again, maybe I'm wrong. You should do your own research and decide for yourself. The more research that I do on this topic, however, the more I become convinced that (with the exception of the oldest of old, and rarest of rare coins) the entire numismatics business is little more than a con job. Therefore, I urge you to do you research before jumping in.

If you're going to buy numismatics, you should do it as a hobby. Buy them because you like them, not as an investment, and you'll never be disappointed. Get to know your local coin shops (there are some very good dealers out there that are honest and well respected), join a club (there are hundreds of them), and learn as much as you can. If you do, your hobby may end up paying off like it was an investment. But if it doesn't, you won't care.

Treachery, Fraud, Scams, Cons, Rackets, Swindles, Hoodwinking, Chicanery, Flimflammery, and Bamboozlement!

In the precious metals sector most of the dealers are honest, hardworking, good people. However, there are also a lot of cons and scams to watch out for. I have condensed for you here a few examples of the best, most creative cons to give you an idea of what to look for. But be warned, it's going to be different each time, and though these examples are creative, there will always be some cunning individual who comes along and shatters the old record of corruption, taking double dealing to a whole new level.

PHONE SCAMS

One of the largest rare coin scams came to light when, on May 24, 2001, the New York attorney general announced the indictment of six New York residents and five corporations for running a rare coin scam that defrauded investors out of at least $25 million.

It appears that six people who jointly owned five corporations, and opened five separate high-pressure telephone boiler room operations, were marketing rare numismatic coins nationwide.

They would pressure customers into buying these rare numismatic coins. Of course the salespeople would lie about the rarity and condition of the coins, but if a customer had any doubts the salesperson would give the customer the phone numbers of several of their competitors so that the customer could get an "independent" appraisal. Little did the customer know that the company the coins were purchased from and all the competing coin shops were not actually competing . . . they all shared the same owners. Needless to say, the "competing" coin shops would always give an appraisal higher than the customer had paid, even though the true value was only 10 percent to 20 percent of what the customer had been charged.

The attorney general's office estimates that more than 1,000 victims lost more than $25 million, with twenty people losing over $100,000 each, and several losing more than $750,000.

TV AND MAGAZINE ADS

Avoid TV and magazine offers like the plague. There's just not enough profit in the precious metals field to support this type of advertising. Wait a minute, let me rephrase that. There is not enough profit for a dealer who is offering *fairly priced* precious metals to support this type of advertising.

As I've mentioned, the normal profit margin on collector coins can range from 15 percent to 100 percent, and the profit on bullion bars and coins can range from 1 percent to 5 percent. So I'll say it again, there is simply not enough profit on precious metals to pay for this type of advertising, unless, of course, you're paying way too much.

Think about this for a minute. If you are advertising in a printed magazine, the magazine will usually require your ad to be in their office at least sixty days before the issue hits the newsstands. The cost that the dealer is paying for bullion varies minute by minute with the worldwide spot price of the precious metals. Silver will often vary by more than 5 percent in a single day, and there was a sixty-day period in 2006 where silver rose by 55 percent.

Now, if you're a dealer planning on selling bullion in magazine ads, and you have to print a price today for precious metals that you're going to sell more than a month from now in a market that is trending higher, and you are planning on selling at a fair markup (1 to 5 percent), then you're planning on losing money. Unless, of course, you have an alternate plan, or should I say, ulterior motive.

If you call that 1-800 number, they're going to try their hardest to switch you into some other very overpriced, supposedly rare numismatic coins, commemorative coins, or other scam. And by the way, unless you've got caller ID blocking, you just gave them your phone number.

COMMEMORATIVE COINS

Another popular precious metals scam is the commemorative coin. When you see them offered on TV or in magazine ads, something is fishy. It's almost certainly a scam.

I can think of no better example of commemorative coin scams than the coin that received the honor of being named "Stupid Investment of the Week" by CBS MarketWatch: the 2004 Freedom Tower Silver Dollar.

Back in 2004, the National Collector's Mint, Inc. began an extensive nationwide TV and magazine ad campaign for the 2004 Freedom Tower Silver Dollar. The ads claimed the coin to be a "legally authorized government issue silver dollar" and a "U.S. territorial minting" from the Commonwealth of the Northern Mariana Islands. They also implied that the coins were made of pure silver from silver bars recovered at Ground Zero.

This prompted an immediate response from the U.S. Mint:

> *The Freedom Tower Silver Dollar is not a genuine United States Mint coin or medal.* Under the Constitution, Congress has the exclusive power to coin money of the United States. . . . Clearly, the Commonwealth of the Northern Mariana Islands, a U.S. insular possession, does not have the authority to coin its own money. . . . Congress did not authorize the National Collector's Mint product, and the United States Government does not endorse it.

The New York attorney general once again rode to the rescue, obtaining a court order to halt sales of the Freedom Tower Silver Dollar, and filed suit against National Collector's Mint for making fraudulent and misleading claims.

In the suit, it was shown that the coins were not made of pure or solid silver, but rather an inexpensive metal alloy plated with approximately one ten-thousandth of an inch of silver valued at approximately 1.4 cents. The attorney general also went on to show that the coins were not legal tender, and that far from being a U.S. territorial minting in the Commonwealth of the Northern Mariana Islands, the coins had actually been minted in Wyoming.

National Collector's Mint had to pay $369,510 in civil penalties, and offer a refund to anyone who purchased the coins. The company ended up paying out $2.2 million in refunds.

But all that publicity did not go to waste. Not missing the opportunity, the coin is now being offered as "the world's most talked about commemorative," and the brand-new 2005 Freedom Tower Dollar is being promoted as "non-circulating Cook Islands legal tender." You've got to admire their tenacity, I guess.

COUNTERFEITS

This is another shady scam that revolves almost exclusively around numismatics.

Almost 99 percent of all counterfeit coins are counterfeit numismatics, not bullion coins. This makes perfect sense because a bullion coin's value is derived solely from its metal content, and a counterfeiter must therefore counterfeit the metal (substitute a far less expensive metal for the precious metal) to make a profit on the coin. This makes the counterfeiter's job incredibly difficult, if not nearly impossible, because he must duplicate the color, density (weight per volume), and sound (ring) of the specific metal he is trying to duplicate in order to pass it off as authentic to the unsuspecting buyer.

Numismatic coins, on the other hand, derive their value from qualities that are far easier to replicate, like the specific design, rarity, age, and condition. Therefore they can be made of the same metal as the original coin, making if far easer to duplicate the original look, sound, and feel.

A very large number of counterfeit numismatic coins don't start out as counterfeits. They start out as legally minted reproduction coins, which are first sold as replicas. Sometimes, however, the original purchaser of the coin resells it, claiming it to be an original, and then the coin becomes counterfeit.

Other coins are manufactured with the express purpose of being passed off as the genuine article. There is currently a flood of these counterfeits coming out of Asia.

Another scam is counterfeit certified coins. Recently I read about people buying certified and slabbed coins online only to find they've been scammed. There are a few ways to do this. The scammer will take some real, high-quality, collectible coins, and send them into a grading service. When he gets them back, the scammer removes the coins from their supposedly tamper-proof slab, and replaces the coins with either real coins of a far lower grade or counterfeits; or the scammer buys his own slabs direct from the manufacturer and then inserts anything he wants. This has been made quite easy as slabs are now available online for less than $2 each.

There is a tremendous advantage for the scammer in selling you a slabbed counterfeit, because you can't hold the coin in your hand, feel the weight and density, and hear the ring of the metal.

DO YOUR DUE DILIGENCE!

So now I'm going to say it one more time: If you're going to buy collector coins, please, please, please do your due diligence and develop a relationship with a dealer you've researched. If you buy from a reputable dealer there should be nothing to worry about other than the buy/sell spread (aka bid/ask spread).

Confiscation

Remember when we talked about how the U.S. government made private ownership of gold illegal in 1933? Well, if you think that can't happen again, think again.

It all comes down to this: The government makes the rules, changes the rules, and enforces the rules. Though it lacks the moral right, it can create the legal authority. Though it lacks the constitutional empowerment, it can turn a blind eye to the Constitution. The Constitution says that only gold and silver coin can be money in the United States, yet they outlawed money and stuck us with currency. The Constitution did not stop the government from taking people's gold in 1933. If the government chooses to outlaw private gold ownership again, there is unfortunately nothing you or I will be able to do about it.

Many times, shady coin dealers will tell you that they sell certain coins that are exempt from confiscation. The whole concept is perpetuated by unscrupulous dealers trying to instill fear in your heart so that they can line their own pockets. If you fall for it, you're going to buy the wrong coins at the wrong price. If the dealer even mentions "nonconfiscatable," then walk out the door, hang up, or move on to the next Web site. This topic comes up time after time and basically the whole thing is a bunch of baloney . . . there is no such thing as something the government can't confiscate. The very fact that a dealer would use the term "nonconfiscatable" is a good tip-off as to what he or she is up to. In my discussion of FDR's policies, I gave you a synopsis of the "nationalization" and "outlawing" of privately held gold, but I never used the word "confiscate," because that isn't what happened.

As proof of my allegations against these unscrupulous dealers, I offer you this one simple fact. The pre-1933 gold coins that they are claiming are nonconfiscatable are the very same coins that the government nationalized. These coins are just the 77 percent of the coins that escaped nationalization because the public retained them, illegally.

Could the government nationalize gold and outlaw its use and private ownership again? Absolutely! Is it likely? Who cares? Not me. I don't worry about it. I plan on it. Then if it happens, I've already covered my basis. But if it doesn't happen, well that's even better.

The government will only nationalize gold and silver if people are asking for them in payment. If people are asking for gold and silver in payment, it means that we are in the midst of a hyperinflation. If we are in a hyperinflation, the vast bulk of the wealth transfer will have already occurred, and it will have been mind-boggling huge. So just sell the government your precious metals and buy something tangible right away (like lots and lots of real estate), before the currency becomes worthless.

Foreign Coins

Here's another con job dealers will use to make a few more bucks off you. Old foreign coins are also often promoted as being "nonconfiscatable" and as you know from our discussion in this chapter, it's a bunch of bull. But the gold in foreign coins is just as good as the gold in domestic coins, right? So what's the problem? Plenty! Here are the three most notable areas of concern:

1. Any numismatic premium associated with foreign coins diminishes outside the country of origin. So if you bought some British Gold Sovereigns, French Gold Roosters, or Danish Gold Mermaids, when it comes time to sell, if you want to get the best price, you're going to have to find buyers in Great Britain, France, and Denmark. Then you're going to have to ship the coins there.

2. Foreign coins are usually oddball weights of gold like 0.2354 troy ounce, and almost never one troy ounce. Also, being a legal tender coin, they're stamped with a denomination like "20 Franks" but they're never stamped with their gold content or purity. This makes it hard to exchange them for anything, or sell them to anybody but a professional, because the average person won't know how much gold they contain, so they don't know what they are worth.

3. The wording on the coins is in the language of the country of origin.

These three factors make foreign coins much more difficult to sell when it comes time, and almost useless in an emergency.

Gold and Silver Pyramids

Network marketing, or multilevel marketing companies, sometimes provide great products at a reasonable price and are usually perfectly legitimate businesses that can offer you the opportunity to make a substantial income from home. However, many people will mask what is nothing more than a pyramid scheme, or should I say scam, in multilevel clothing. Pyramid schemes are illegal, and by their very nature impoverish almost nine people for each one person they enrich.

By their very nature pyramid schemes (sometimes called snowballs) require that there be a very large number of losers for each big winner. It's a road to riches for the few, but a pathway to poverty for the many. Several of these have already sprung up in the precious metals field, and I'm sure there will be dozens more before this bull market is over. Steer clear, and don't buy in.

IRS Reporting Requirements

REPORTING REQUIREMENTS OF PRECIOUS METALS PURCHASES
(when you buy)
Here are the requirements for reporting your precious metal purchases to the government: There are none.

There is no limit to the amount of precious metals you can own, and neither the dealer nor the customer is required to report the purchase of any precious metal, in any quantity, period. If the IRS wanted to know exactly who is buying precious metals they'd have a form for reporting it. They don't. Don't fall for the scams.

REPORTING OF CASH TRANSACTIONS (when you buy or sell)
The government couldn't care less about precious metals transactions—unless they are in large chunks of cash. They're really, really interested if you're making purchases with large amounts of cash because it makes you look like a terrorist, drug dealer, member of organized crime, or maybe you're not paying

your taxes. Just try going into your local Lamborghini dealer with a suitcaseful of cash and see what happens.

Any transaction (or two or more related transactions) involving cash (or cash equivalents) in amounts of $10,000 or greater must be reported to the IRS by the seller. Again, the dealer must report the *cash*, not the precious metals.

The way I deal with all of this is that I will not take any cash, ever. I deal only by bank wire transfer. There are millions upon millions of them every day and some are for billions of dollars. The banks don't report them, and precious metals dealers aren't required to either.

REPORTING OF SALES *(when you sell)*

If you decide to cash out, and you want to sell your precious metals stash back to your dealer, some items require dealer reporting and some do not.

The IRS is somewhat vague here, but their rules seem to have a bizarre fascination with items that were traded as commodities contracts back in the 1980s.

According to the IRS, the sale of any of these items, in one transaction, requires your dealer to file form 1099B reporting the transaction of:

- 25 or more, 1-ounce Gold Maple Leafs, Krugerrands, or Mexican Onzas
- 1 or more, 1-kilo (32.15 troy ounces) gold bars
- 1 or more, 100-ounce gold bars

However, due to the vagueness of the IRS rules, the Industry Council for Tangible Assets (ICTA) interprets the rules more broadly. According to the ICTA, your dealer is required to report on sales of the above mentioned items, plus:

- Any size gold bar totaling 1 kilo (32.15 troy ounces) or more
- Any size platinum bar totaling 25 troy ounces or more
- Any size palladium bar totaling 100 troy ounces or more
- Any size silver bar totaling 1,000 troy ounces or more
- And any combination of 90 percent silver coins totaling $1,000 face value or more

Dealer reporting requirements do not apply to American Gold Eagles or Silver Eagles no matter the quantities. Furthermore, reporting requirements do not apply to any fractional (less than an ounce) gold coins. This also extends to foreign coins, as well as commemorative coins and medallions. In other words, if it's not on the list, it's not reported.

But none of these dealer reportable sales really matter because:

1. If you were worried about reporting because you don't want anyone (even the government) to know that you have gold and silver, stop worrying. Even if you bought reportable items, by the time your sale gets reported, you no longer have those items.
2. If you're playing by the rules, and you made a capital gain, *you* are required to report that gain whether your dealer reported it or not. That's something we'll cover briefly in the next section.

All of the rules above are as of the writing of this book. But remember, the government makes the rules, changes the rules, and enforces the rules. And when it finally comes time to sell, you need to consult your tax advisor.

REPORTING OF CAPITAL GAINS *(after you sell)*

Just as with stocks, bonds, and other investments, you are obligated to report your capital gains to the IRS when it comes to precious metals. Don't make the mistake of confusing your dealer's reporting obligation with your reporting obligation. If you made a capital gain, the IRS wants to know about it. So keep all your receipts and records, and get proper tax advice from a professional.

For those who want to make their own rules, I have but these few words: If you choose to play cat and mouse with the government, it will serve you well to remember just who is the mouse.

Get proper tax advice.

Chapter 15

Who Are You, and What's Your Plan?

"The secret to your financial success is inside yourself. If you become a critical thinker who takes no Wall Street "fact" on faith, and you invest with patient confidence, you can take steady advantage of even the worst bear markets. By developing your discipline and your courage, you can refuse to let other people's mood swings govern your financial destiny. In the end, how your investments behave is much less important than how you behave."

BENJAMIN GRAHAM

Before you invest, it will be a lot easier, more productive, and far less stressful if you first decide what your ultimate goals are and then figure out the best way to get there. It's not enough to say, "My goal is to make a lot of money." If you jump in without a well-defined goal and plan to get there, you're asking for a lot of anxiety and grief. I've seen people jump in and out, buy and sell, take a full position in physical metals, then decide mining stocks were better, and then panic and sell after reading a newsletter saying there could be a downturn.

If you believe in the case that I've made for cycles, and if you intend on becoming a cycles investor, then by definition you should be in it for the duration of the cycle. Don't get spooked at every downturn and don't change course midstream.

I used to constantly worry whether I had done the right thing when it came to my investments. In 2002 and early 2003, in the portfolios that I control for a few select friends and family members, I allocated about 80 percent of those funds to the precious metals sector. In 2004 and 2005 real estate was the hot sector, and for a brief moment I wondered, "Should I invest these funds in real estate instead of precious metals?" Then I came to my senses. I looked at all my research and said, "This real estate craze is just a bubble in a cycle that has matured over the last twenty years."

As I write this the subprime lending market is blowing up, central banks across the globe are coming to the rescue with helicopter drops of hundreds of billions of dollars, and many of the buyers that jumped in at the top are getting slaughtered. In fact, on March 11, 2008, the Fed swooped in with an unprecedented $200 billion bailout for the financial industry by allowing institutions to swap out risky mortgage-backed securities for federally backed bonds. As you've probably guessed by now, the Fed doesn't have the money on hand for this. So where will it come from? Thin air. Just like that, 200 billion more dollars will be added to an economy where the dollar is becoming a laughingstock already. This will, of course, cause even more inflationary pressure on the dollar and is just one more example of the Fed passing the costs of big business mistakes on to you and me in the form of their favorite hidden tax—inflation.

In 2005–2006, I again started doubting myself as base metals such as nickel, lead, and zinc began outperforming precious metals. I watched them soar, but I remembered my plan and the fact that base metals are not money, they'll never be money, and if the economy deflates, base metals will head south for the winter.

You Need a Plan!

The more I study, the more I am absolutely convinced that there is no better place to be for this portion of the cycle than in precious metals. I never doubt my choices anymore, and every question I come up with always has the same answer: Investing in precious metals is the safest and smartest investment for my plan. Develop a plan, write it down, and stick with it. A little later in this section I'll share my plan with you.

Just because you write down a plan, however, doesn't mean you can't modify it. Continuously refining and clarifying your plan is a good thing, and if you discover that your plan is flawed, then modification is a must. Success or failure can hinge on not only the quality of your plan, but also the continual refinement and execution of it.

A good investment plan will help you stay the course, thus increasing your chance of success. The professionals use greed and fear to manipulate the market. Riding the bull and staying in the game can be difficult. It's often referred to as "climbing a wall of worry." If you have a clearly defined written plan, you can refer to it when you have doubts, and you will be far more likely to investigate those doubts by doing proper research and due diligence instead of making a rash decision.

A plan should have a goal, a strategy (the big picture of how you're going to get from A to B), and a tactic (the specific methods to be employed to implement the strategy).

As an example, here's my plan:

GOAL
To accumulate X number of high-cash-flow apartment buildings.

STRATEGY
Invest with the cycles and identify the top-performing investments in each cycle. My research has shown a high probability that precious metals will be the top performers of the current market cycle.

TACTIC
In the first phase of my strategy I will employ the tactic of investing in the precious metals sector. My core position will be in physical metals, heavily weighted toward silver. I will achieve leverage through a position in a large basket of mining and exploration stocks. I will leverage myself further by starting a business that I believe will prosper in the economic environment I foresee. I will also prepare for the second phase of my strategy by continuing my

education on real estate investing. I will continue my quest, as a cycle investor, to educate myself and to be vigilant, so as to identify when this cycle tops out and prepare for the next cycle change.

Develop Your Plan

To develop an investment plan that is right for you, you first need to ask yourself, *Who am I?* Take a look at your own personality and determine what kind of an investor you are. Here are some good questions to ask yourself:

- What is my risk tolerance?
- Am I a trader or an investor?
- How actively involved do I want to be with my investments?
- What is more important to me: the potential for huge gains, or a good night's sleep?
- Am I young or old?
- Am I investing to build wealth now, or for retirement? If I am already re-tired, am I looking for safety and potential growth, or do I need income?

As of the writing of this book, I'm convinced that precious metals should offer huge gains *and* a good night's sleep. In fact, for me, it's the only investment that gives a good night's sleep.

Once you have answered these questions, you can then define your goal and develop a strategy to get you there.

Here's a worksheet to help you. Circle one choice for each category. If there's a category I left out that's important to you, add it. This should help you figure out what strategy is best to get you to your goal.

For example, regarding the reason for investing, if you circled "1, Need Income," then stop reading this book and go find some cash-flowing real estate. Gold and silver do not cash-flow, and very few mining stocks pay dividends.

Of these categories, I think the most important are the "risk tolerance" and "involvement" categories. If you know your risk tolerance and the level of involvement you're willing to take on, then deciding how you will invest in precious metals becomes much easier.

Risk Tolerance

Safety	1	2	3	4	5	6	7	8	9	10	Thrills
Physical Metals	–	Mutual Funds	–	Big Stocks	–	Small Stocks	–	Futures and Options			

Involvement

None	1	2	3	4	5	6	7	8	9	10	Daily
Investor					Swing Trader						Day Trader

Reason for Investing

Need	1	2	3	4	5	6	7	8	9	10	Future
Income											Wealth

Age

Old	1	2	3	4	5	6	7	8	9	10	Young

Portfolio Size

Large	1	2	3	4	5	6	7	8	9	10	Small

The type of investor you are has even more impact on the amount of work required than the type of investment you choose. I believe that an investor who takes a position early and hangs on for the ride has a far greater chance of reaping huge rewards than a trader who is trying to buy the dips and sell the peaks because inevitably there will come a day when you sell on what you perceive to be a peak. But then the peak turns out not to be a peak at all, just a slight plateau, and the price takes off again as you wait for the next pullback. By the time the peak finally comes, the profits that you didn't make due to cashing out early cancel out all the profits you gained by not riding through the downturns . . . and then some. The result is that you will have magnified the amount of time and effort expended, only to reduce your potential return.

Physical precious metals are, by far, the safest and least amount of work of any investment in the precious metals sector, and they still offer the potential for enormous gains. Just buy them now, sit on them until they have become overvalued and go into a bubble, then sell.

Because physical metals are such an incredibly safe, no-brainer investment, they have made up at lease 50 percent to 70 percent of the allocation in the portfolios that I control since 2003. For some of my customers who have less risk tolerance, and are especially concerned about the U.S. dollar, I sometimes recommend their portfolios contain 75 percent, or even 100 percent, physical precious metals, and, as I said before, I'm heavily biased toward silver. But don't just take my word for it. Do your research, and make the investment decisions you think best suit your goals.

Mining stocks and mutual funds introduce risk, whereas gold and silver cannot go bankrupt. A mine can have labor disputes, permit and licensing problems, can be shut down by environmental agencies (like the EPA), and can suffer from bad management, bad bookkeeping, and a host of other problems that never seem to quit, including nationalization. Many mines are located in countries that have histories of economic problems and military coups.

Nonetheless, I like mining stocks. If you want to leverage the metals, use the mining stocks. The junior mining stocks can give you big leverage, but with that leverage comes risk, though I believe the large-cap stocks actually offer more safety and less risk than mutual funds. For instance, when a mutual fund shows a profit, management and everyone else at the fund get paid first, and you get what's left over. When a mutual fund suffers a loss, however, they still get paid and then pass the loss, plus management fees, on to you. Mutual funds are less work than stocks, but not by much. All you need for the stocks is a trading account, and some good information.

Trading stocks, however, can be a dangerous game. When investing in stocks, if you are confident in your investment (and you should only invest if you are confident), you need to stay in for the long haul. Before I wrote down my plan, there were a couple of times that I gave in to greed and fear, and sold a portion of my position in large-cap mining stocks. I listened to some "good" technical analysts who were predicting a severe pullback in mining stocks. I panicked, fearing I'd lose some of the profits I had made, and succumbed to greed, thinking I could later buy back my precious metals stakes at a lower price. Each time fate and the markets conspired to punish me, and they gave me a sound thrashing that I will never forget.

The market took off like a rocket, doing exactly the opposite of what these "experts" were predicting. As the mining stock prices climbed higher and higher, my fear of buying back in and then seeing the analysts' predictions of a crash finally come true, causing even bigger losses, kept me from reentering the market.

When I finally did buy back in, it was at far higher prices. So I couldn't buy nearly as many shares as I had sold. When I added up the tax loss and the gains that I missed while I was not fully invested, I was horrified. The shares that I had sold had done very well previously, so the sale was a taxable event. My holdings in the shares that I traded would have been double what they are today had I not traded, and I wouldn't have faced the tax exposure I incurred. This was my punishment for not having my plan written down, and for not following my plan. I will never again trade or sell based on technical analysis. Technical analysis is right 55 percent or 60 percent of the time, but the fundamentals are right 100 percent of the time, and always, always, always prove themselves over time.

Write your plan down and follow it. When you have doubts, read it.

Warren Buffett once said, "Put all your eggs in one basket and then watch that basket very carefully." That to me is very sound advice. By going 80 percent or more into precious metals and precious metals mining stocks, I have put all my eggs in one basket. But in order to ensure my investment strategy is successful, I need to watch my basket carefully, always reevaluating my strategy to maximize my returns.

I'm comfortable with my plan, it fits me like a warm sweater and a pair of old shoes. The only time my plan didn't work for me was when I didn't follow it. So I subscribe to several newsletters, and when they recommend an investment, I do my due diligence and then buy it if it fits my plan and I think the fundamentals are good.

A Good Team Is Part of a Good Plan

As Robert Kiyosaki says, "Investing is a team sport." He also says, "Hire the best advisors and pay them well."

How do you hire a team to help you make investment choices in the precious metals sector?

The simplest way to put together a great team is to subscribe to some great newsletters. However, you should get recommendations first, because some newsletters are not so great. You can get recommendations from the other parts of your team. And the other parts of your team don't necessarily have to be people. They can be investment books such as this one, or any of the Rich Dad books (many will have a resources section in the back), and financial Web sites that specialize in the precious metals sector. Many good sources are listed in the resources section of this book. Start reading them to educate yourself, and you will slowly gravitate toward the better newsletter writers that fit your style.

In 2001, I started studying the stock markets and the global economy. By 2002 I had put together my team and had studied the precious metals sector enough to know that precious metals had finished their twenty-year bear market and were just beginning a new long-term bull market, and that the stock and real estate bull markets were dead. I started buying gold at $300 per ounce, and silver at $4.10. As of this writing gold is selling for nearly $1,000 an ounce, and silver is selling for almost $20 an ounce.

I am so grateful that I found my team and listened to their advice early in this bull market.

So, now that I've shared my plan with you, what's yours?

Chapter 16

Let's Get Physical

A lot of people fall into the trap of thinking that they don't have to physically own their precious metals. Either they think they can leverage their position better by buying mining stocks, or they think the futures contracts or ETFs they own are as good as gold. As I've mentioned, that's just plain stinking thinking.

First off, if you're reasoning, "Mining stocks give me leverage; I'll just buy the stocks," then think again. First, if everyone just bought mining stocks, and no one bought physical gold and silver, then the price of gold and silver wouldn't rise. In fact, it would fall because of lack of demand, while all the extra funds available to the mining sector because everyone was buying their stock would then spur increased supply. Second, mining stocks are *stocks*. They are *not* gold and silver. They are shares in a *company* that processes gold or silver. As such, they are subject to market conditions such as a currency crisis or stock market crash. Gold and silver, on the other hand, could rocket to the moon while the mining stocks fall.

But beyond that there are a number of reasons physically owning gold and silver is the ultimate way to invest for this part of the cycle that we are in. They are:

1. For 5,000 years, gold and silver have been the only assets that have never failed. Because they are tangible assets of inherent value their purchasing power will never fall to zero.

2. They are financial assets that can be completely private and not part of the financial system. Even real estate requires the financial system to transfer title. Gold and silver do not.

3. They are one of the few financial assets that are not simultaneously someone else's liability. Stocks, bonds, and derivatives like futures and ETFs require the performance of the issuer or counterparty. Even cash requires the performance of the government that issues it to have value. If a government fails, so does its currency. Gold and silver never fail.

4. They can be wholly owned. You can never really own real estate for instance; if you think you can, just try not paying your property taxes for a few years.

5. They are safe-haven investments that rise during economic upheaval, war, terrorism, and natural disaster.

6. They have a proven track record of performing well in inflation or deflation.

7. They have a high value density. That means that, unlike copper or oil, a very small amount of gold or silver provides significant purchasing power.

8. They have a low bid/ask spread, unlike diamonds or collector coins, which can carry a 15 percent to 100 percent spread.

9. Every ounce has the same value. Every diamond or collector coin, on the other hand, is different and requires an expert to assess the value.

10. Physical gold and silver are money in and of themselves.

It is my recommendation that you establish a core physical position of gold- and silver-before you ever diversify into mining stocks, futures, options, ETFs, or any other gold- and silver-related investment. Every precious metals investor should have a core position of physical gold and silver that they do not trade. A core position can be held many ways. The size of your core position will be a major factor in determining the different ways it is held. Here are a few.

Go to the Mattresses

As I've mentioned, the first thing you want to do to buy precious metals is to find a trustworthy dealer that will give you good services and advice. To purchase physical gold and silver there are basically two kinds of dealers to choose from: online bullion dealers or coin shops.

As in any market, price and service quality vary among dealers, so finding a trustworthy one is a crucial first step. Ideally, there would be several within a short drive. But bullion dealers are scarce, and most bullion is bought online or over the phone and delivered through the mail. Because of the extremely low profit margin on bullion products, I don't know of any bullion-only walk-in shops. For a bullion-only dealer you will have to go online. The easiest way to find these dealers is to Google "gold and silver," and dozens of dealers will come up. I can't stress enough, however, how important it is to do your research before engaging any of the dealers you find online. You can find out more information on my Web site, GoldSilver.com.

Service quality among dealers can vary widely, so you should go to the Better Business Bureau online at bbb.org and do a search to see who's had complaints, who hasn't, and how they were resolved. Also, check to see if the dealer is a member of the Industry Council for Tangible Assets (ICTA). You can do a search by dealer name or by state at ictaonline.org.

Further, when buying online, make sure the final price you are quoted includes shipping, handling, and that it is fully insured all the way till delivery.

Many numismatic coin dealers offer bullion, but because of the low profit margin the coin shops will either charge more than the online dealers, or they will sell bullion to entice you through the door. Once you're inside, they will show you lots of really pretty, really expensive numismatic stuff that you can buy. Before you purchase these coins, go back to the chapter "Beware the Pitfalls" and read the section on numismatics.

Form or Function

One of the most important decisions to make regarding gold and silver in your possession is, *What form should I buy? Bars, old U.S. silver coins, Maple*

Leaves, or U.S. Eagles? To answer that you have to ask why you want to hold gold and/or silver at home in the first place. For most people, the reason to have gold and silver at home is to have a very private investment, and also as an emergency currency and portable wealth.

For storage at home my preference for both gold and silver is U.S. Eagles. They are among the most recognizable forms of gold and silver. They look official and say, "United States of America" and "one troy ounce fine gold" or "one troy ounce fine silver" on them. They are in one-ounce increments (remember you can sell your gold and silver at a coin shop for cash, but when silver goes over $100 per ounce, even a 100-ounce silver bar will be over the cash limit). And lastly, U.S. Eagles are extremely private because there is no reporting requirement when you sell.

Storing Your Gold and Silver

Once you've got your gold and silver you need to decide where you're going to keep your stash. This has always been a problem, and it's a good problem to have, but there is no easy answer.

SAFE DEPOSIT BOX

Many people refer to a safe deposit box as a "safety deposit box." This is incorrect. It is a "box" that you can "deposit" things into, which resides in the "safe" at your bank, in other words, a safe deposit box.

People have a tendency to think the best place to keep gold and silver is in a safe deposit box at the bank, thinking that it really *is* a "safety" box. This may or may not be a good idea; you'll have to decide for yourself. I can tell you this, when the terrorist attacks happened September 11, 2001, gold rose 9 percent, and silver rose 11 percent, but if it was in a bank you couldn't get to it. During that week the stock markets were closed, the banks were closed, and ATMs ran out of cash. But the precious metals dealers were open and you could walk in with your gold or silver, and walk out with $100 bills. The precious metals dealers were the banks that week, but only for those who could get to their gold and silver.

Yet another reason to rethink safe deposit boxes comes from a story my office manager told me. She banks with a major national bank that had made the decision to close her local branch where her account was held, and she was informed that her account would be transferred to a nearby branch. The transition went smoothly, and after several months of banking at the new branch she needed to retrieve something from her safe deposit box. To her horror she was informed that, though her account had been moved to that branch, her safe deposit box had not, and to top it off, the bank had no idea as to which branch it had been moved. The box was eventually found, but not till after a long search.

Lastly, safe deposit boxes are not insured. Most people think FDIC insurance or the bank's insurance covers safe deposit boxes. It does not.

I believe everyone should have gold and silver in his or her own private possession, where you can lay your hands on it, because they are one of the few financial assets that can be completely private and not part of the financial system. Just be aware that if you choose to store your precious metals at the bank, you are exposing the most private of investments to the most public financial and banking systems and the laws that govern them.

Some alternative options to consider are:

A HIDDEN FLOOR SAFE OR WALL SAFE

You may also want to discuss this with your insurance agent first, but if you want to store any significant amount of gold or silver at home, a good safe is a good investment. Talk to a professional safe company.

VAULT STORAGE

If you decide that you aren't comfortable with storing your gold or silver at home, there are several different types of storage accounts available for precious metals at various levels of security.

Segregated Vault Storage. This is the highest level of security available, and I have experience with this because my company offers this type of storage at Brink's. (Yes, this is the same Brink's that has the armored cars that deliver the currency to the banks.) Brink's is not part of the banking system and does not fall under the same laws and jurisdiction as the banks. During the week of 9/11, the government shut down the banking system, but Brink's was still open, doing business, and shipping and receiving gold and silver. In fact, they are open 364 days a year (they only close on Christmas Day). Many dealers can provide service similar to this.

Once the funds are received for your order, your gold and silver will be counted under the watchful eye of an auditor and under videotape surveillance. The counter and the auditor both have to sign an inventory list, and then your precious metals are placed into a container and sealed. They are then tagged with your name, account number, the contents, and securely stored in the vault.

If you ever want your metals shipped to you, just call and they will be on their way within forty-eight hours (excluding weekends). Even if ten years have passed, you will receive the exact same bars and coins that you purchased.

Another advantage is that when you want to sell your metals back, they're already in the vault system. So they don't need to be recertified by an expert (saving the associated charges). It's liquid, and it's quick. There's no time lost in transit because they're already in the vault. When you sell, your check will usually be mailed, or a bank wire transfer completed within seventy-two hours. Sometimes if you sell back to the dealer in the early morning, funds can be wire-transferred into your account and cleared (available to write a check against) in as little as twenty-four hours.

The holdings are allocated to you and are not carried as an asset on the dealer's books. Should the dealer change ownership, file bankruptcy, or close for any reason, your precious metals are still safe. They are still yours. Visit GoldSilver.com for more information.

Allocated Vault Storage. This is the second highest level of storage security. Allocated vault storage guarantees that there are ounces of silver or gold in the vault allocated to you, but not any particular ounces. The forms of gold and silver that are used in allocated storage are usually large, and cost-effective. When you sell, allocated accounts are usually settled in cash. If you ever want to take delivery, your metal will be delivered as a large bar, or you will most likely pay a fee to have it converted to the form you prefer.

Let's Get Virtual

I'm going to group together here any kind of gold or silver that can be bought and sold instantly over the Internet, that you can never see or touch, and that claims to be stored in fully insured vault storage. Many of these we've already discussed throughout this book, so I won't get too detailed.

EXCHANGE-TRADED FUNDS (ETFS)

Exchange-traded funds are the most well known form of "digital gold" and were covered in earlier in the "Beware the Pitfalls" chapter, where I cautioned against ETFs. Though they claim to have "allocated" metals, you must remember, even if they have the metals, they are allocated to the ETF, and not you. Another thing to consider is that the ETFs are run by, and therefore part of, the banking system. So if you use the ETFs, you are playing their game.

However, if you are going to trade gold or silver, rather than hold it as a long-term investment, then these are the vehicles for you. They have, by far, the narrowest bid/ask spread, highest liquidity, and can be bought and sold just like a stock on any trading platform. Their stock ticker symbols are GLD for gold and SLV for silver.

DIGITAL BULLION TRADING EXCHANGES

There are several bullion trading exchanges available to investors. Digital bullion exchanges store precious metals, and their customers trade the metals within this private exchange system.

The customer goes to the exchange Web site, creates an account, and funds the account by means of bank wire transfer. You must also verify your identity. Once the account is funded you can buy metals at competitive prices. You can't trade metals on these private exchanges through the trading platform or brokerage account that you may currently be using. Instead, you must log on to their Web site and trade within their system. That means you are not trading on the world markets, but instead you are trading with the other customers within the system. Therefore, pricing can be different from global open market pricing.

DIGITAL PRECIOUS METALS CURRENCY

Digital precious metals currency is an online method used to instantly buy or sell gold and silver, twenty-four hours a day, seven days a week, 365 days a year. It's easy, the storage fees are very low, and it can also be used to pay in gold anyone who has an e-mail address.

I can speak from personal experience here as I have used one of these companies for some time now.

Having an account at the company I deal with is sort of like having a bank account, currency trading account, payment system, and bullion storage account, all in one. You can hold any combination of, and/or trade between, U.S. dollars, euros, British pounds, Canadian dollars, gold, and silver. While holding these currencies you are paid interest at a rate comparable with a savings account, and, when holding gold or silver, your storage and account fees are among the most competitive in the industry. The metals are allocated and at all times vested to, and owned by, the customer. So you are the absolute owner of your gold and silver . . . no one else.

I believe this is the best way to hold precious metals outside your own country. As always, however, do your due diligence before engaging a company. You can find more information on these types of companies at GoldSilver.com

GOLD AND SILVER IN YOUR IRA

If your IRA is one of your primary investment vehicles, you might be wondering if there is a way to store gold or silver in it. There are two ways to hold gold and silver in your IRA: through ETF shares or through allocated storage.

Since ETFs are traded on public exchanges like stocks, you can have your IRA administrator purchase them to become part of your portfolio.

If you wish to utilize allocated storage for your IRA, you will need to make sure that the company administering your IRA will allow you to invest in physical bullion. If your IRA company does not allow you to invest in precious metals, then you will need to establish an IRA account with a custodian who will hold your precious metal investments. Once you have an account with one of them, most precious metals dealers can fill your order. Then a custodian (usually a major bank) will hold your metals in allocated storage, and you will receive a monthly statement. Visit GoldSilver.com for more information.

A Few Last Words

Once again, in the portfolios that I control, physical precious metals constitute about 50 percent to 70 percent of the investments. Roughly 20 percent to 40 percent is allocated to precious metals stocks, 5 percent to 10 percent is divided between energy stocks and stocks in other commodities, and the remaining 5 percent is cash (you know what I think of cash). So far this has served me well.

The mixture of physical metals that I prefer for the at home portion of my physical allocation is 10 percent to 50 percent gold, and 50 percent to 90 percent silver. The quantity you keep at home depends on the size of your investment, but it's typically somewhere between 3 to 100 ounces of gold, and 100 to 10,000 ounces of silver. Whatever the amount, the idea is to have it close at hand where it can be accessed at any time, no matter the economic or political circumstances.

Of my remaining physical metals, I store a good portion in various security storage locations in the U.S and then the rest in an offshore account. To me, there is safety in geographical diversity.

One more thing regarding silver: Always buy 0.999 fine silver. This is what I call "investment grade" silver. It's the silver that industry needs, and with the world running low on supply, it is the silver they will pay dearly for. *Do not* buy old U.S. 90 percent silver coins (unless you collect them as a hobby) or other forms of un-pure silver such as sterling silver.

If you sell silver that is not 0.999 fine back to a dealer, the dealer will usually sell it to a refinery. Between 1979 and 1981, when silver's price was quite high, so many people were selling so much old silverware, jewelry, and such along with 90 percent silver coins, that all of the silver refiners got jammed up for more than a year. I'm pretty sure that this will happen again, and if it does, your junk silver might sell at a significant discount to pure silver.

One of the things I love most about buying physical gold and silver for storage at home, segregated storage at a depository, and/or offshore storage in an allocated account, is that you are not playing their game, meaning the corporate financial industry game. Instead you are keeping your money and your investments private, away from prying eyes. You know that what you have in your possession is real. You can touch it. And best of all, it's real money.

Chapter 17

Everything Is Illuminated in the Light of the Past

"Although history never quite repeats itself, and just because no development is inevitable, we can in a measure learn from the past to avoid a repetition of the same process. One need not be a prophet to be aware of impending dangers. An accidental combination of experience and interest will often reveal events to one man under aspects which few yet see."

F. A. Hayek, *The Road to Serfdom*, 1944

Whether you like it or not, the empire of the United States of America is now in decline. Yes, the U.S. is an empire. Our military presence and might reaches around the globe, and the U.S. is the only nation on earth that because of the dollar's status as the reserve currency of the world, has the ability to tax, through currency creation, all other nations.

History, it seems, is always doomed to repeat itself, and just as with all empires before it, in the midst of increasing economic uncertainty, Americans have been participating in a fire sale of their freedoms in the process. It should be clear by now that the U.S. is no different than ancient Greece, Rome, or any other empire that funded its expansion through fiat currency creation.

Public works, social programs, and war, paid for by deficit spending, it's a lethal mix, and it always has been. Throughout time, it has brought about the demise of empires. For this, and a myriad of other reasons, the dollar's days as the reserve currency of the world, and thus America's ability to dictate world economic policy through fiat currency creation, are numbered.

And I'm not the only "lunatic" saying so. During Ben Bernanke's testimony to the Joint Economic Committee of Congress on November 8, 2007, Senator Charles Schumer commented, "Quite frankly, I think we are at a moment of economic crisis stemming from four key areas: falling housing prices, lack of confidence in creditworthiness, the weak dollar, and high oil prices. Each of these problems alone would be enough of a threat to our economic well-being. But taken together, they are essentially the four horsemen of economic crisis."

This is all bad news for the U.S., but it is *great* news for precious metals investors. "That's terrible," you say. Yes it is, but the U.S. government insists on destroying the prosperity it once enjoyed. I can't stop them, and neither can you. So we may as well make the best of it and take advantage of the coming wealth transfer.

There used to be a saying that went, "Put 10 percent of your money in gold and pray it doesn't work." In the portfolios I control, I've put 50 percent to 70 percent into the physical metals, 20 percent to 40 percent in mining stocks, and 5 percent to 10 percent in energy stocks. For the sake of the world's standard of living, I pray it doesn't work. I almost hope I go broke, but that's not going to happen. There is an enormous wealth transfer happening now, and it's going to get bigger.

I wish it were not so, but the standard of living, especially in the United States, is about to fall dramatically. As the volatility and economic upheaval progresses, the wealth transfer will increase dramatically. Whether wealth is transferred toward you or away from you is entirely up to you . . . it's your decision. The economy is going to become very bad for most people, but it can become very good for you.

Is it possible the dollar could fail? Times are changing rapidly. Information, ideas, sentiment, knowledge, opinions, and understanding are changing more rapidly than any other time in history, mostly due to the mass media and the Internet. There is an enlightenment going on, and one of the areas of growing awareness and understanding is the immorality of currency creation, and the wealth transfer it causes.

The paradox is that as more people wake up to the fact that currency silently steals wealth from them and then begin rushing to money, massive amounts of wealth are transferred from the latecomers to those who acquired their precious metals early on.

I'm not the only one who thinks it's possible the dollar, and as a result, all fiat currencies, could fail. History gives a zero percent chance of survival to a fiat currency, and today, all the world's currencies are fiat.

So what would the wealth transfer be like if fiat currencies failed? And how would it affect you?

Think of your city. Now try to guess how many people actually have any substantial portion of their wealth in precious metals. Is it one in every 1,000, 2,000, 5,000 or 10,000? Whatever the number is, if the world's currencies were to collapse, the purchasing power of those who don't have precious metals would get transferred to those who do, and that's a mind-bogglingly huge number.

One of the reasons that I wrote this book is because there are some very big players taking enormous positions in precious metals right now. I am concerned that just a small number of big players, who are already "über-rich" anyway, will end up with all the cookies. A wealth transfer of this magnitude could be a road to serfdom for the masses. So I have made it my mission to get as much gold and silver in the hands of as many private investors as possible.

More than any other time in human history, you can increase your standard of living exponentially during this upheaval, without exposing yourself to great risk. Almost all the financial professionals, and even those in the precious metals community, will tell you that precious metals are not an investment, but rather a safe haven. Wealth insurance, if you will.

But while it is true that gold and silver are always, and at all times, *the* safe haven and protection against economic upheaval, there are these ever so brief moments in history where gold and silver are simultaneously the safe heaven insurance, and the best-performing investment of the day, achieving truly massive gains in absolute purchasing power.

This time, however, the coming wealth transfer is set against the backdrop of global imbalances that dwarf any that have come before, coupled with the fact that, for the first time, all the world's currencies are fiat and they are all exhibiting signs of weakness, stress cracks in the global financial system.

It is impossible for me to emphasize enough how incredibly rare this moment in time is. This is not just a once-in-a-lifetime opportunity. It is a once-in-human-existence opportunity, and it will never come again. The coming wealth transfer will be the likes of which the world has never seen. I'm not going out on a limb here if I say that if, after reading this book, you don't take action, you will regret it for the rest of your life.

So will this fight end with the precious metals winning by a technical decision as gold and silver rise to astronomical heights while they do their accounting but still allowing the fiat currencies to survive? Or will it be a knockout blow, and the death of fiat currencies? The difference will decide whether the wealth transfer will be just huge, or absolutely gargantuan. But it really doesn't matter, because: *There is no possible scenario in which gold and silver do not rise.*

The final chart that I'm going to show you is the same as Charts 2, 3, and 4, the Monetary Base plus Revolving Credit versus the dollar value of the U.S. Gold Reserves, only this time the chart extends to 2008. What is truly amazing about this chart is that it clearly shows that the accounting gold has done, time after time, for the last 2,400 years, has begun once again. Just for it to do what it did in 1934 and 1980, gold's dollar price has to exceed $6,900 to account for the Monetary Base plus Revolving Credit Outstanding. And that, my friends, is outstanding!

These are just the figures if they stop printing currency and creating credit today, and if the dollar survives. If the dollar doesn't survive, then the dollar price of gold would be infinite.

Chart 32. Monetary Base & Revolving Credit vs. Gold Reserves 1918–2008

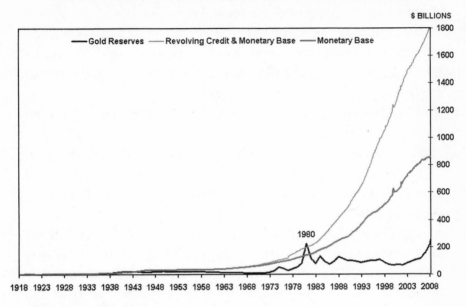

Source: St. Louis Federal Reserve Bank

Clarity of Vision

I've always had 20/10 vision. That means I can see something from twenty feet away just as clearly as the average person can see it from ten feet away. In other words, looking at something from twenty feet, my vision is twice as clear.

I feel privileged that shortly after September 11, 2001, a friend of mine, Cameron Hamza, introduced me to a group of men whose vision was clearer than mine. Men like Richard Russell, Jim Puplava, Jim Rogers, and Marc Faber. I listened to them carefully, and I've been listening to them ever since.

Since the turn of the century these men have been jumping up and down, pointing to the horizon, saying to anyone that would listen, "Look . . . Something is coming." "Where?" we all ask. "Out there, that dot on the horizon. Look, it's huge. Can't you see it?"

The person with average vision cannot see what they see, so they dismiss them, calling them crackpots and such. But I could see a faint blur, so I looked deeper. I studied; I read; I educated myself; and I listened to even more men whose vision was clearer than mine. Men like David Walker, Richard Duncan, and Ron Paul. And as my focus sharpened, I too could see it.

I began to gather more men of clear vision. Men who could show me how to protect myself from what's coming. Men like James Turk, David Morgan, John Embry, Ted Butler, and Ian Gordon. All the men of clear vision then gathered together and formed a human pyramid, then they told me to climb up top so that I could see over the horizon. "There it is!" I shouted. "It's big, and it's really bad. It's the biggest economic storm this planet has ever known, a colossal cyclone, a tempest of unimaginable proportions, and it's headed right for us!"

"Yeah," they said, "we know. We've been trying to tell people for years, but few would listen." It is for the men of clear vision, and for those they are trying to warn, that I write this book. Now I add my voice to theirs.

I met Robert Kiyosaki in 2005. He was holding one of his favorite live events: a book study where 100 to 200 people who have all done their homework by reading the assigned book get together to discuss, analyze, and interpret the book, the world, and their lives. It is always a weekend of revelation and inspiration.

The book we were studying was *The Dollar Crisis* by Richard Duncan. The book outlines how we came to this cliff's edge of financial ruin and how years of fiscal malfeasance had built up an energy that would soon visit its rage upon us as a monetary monsoon of a magnitude yet unknown.

As we studied the crisis, storm clouds darkened the room, the wind whipped the pages of our books, and the rain began pelting our bodies. But in the middle of the storm, Robert was standing there, alone in the sunlight, unruffled by the wind, and untouched by the rain.

"Bring it on!" he yelled. "Real investors don't run from crisis. They run toward it! Bring it on!"

It was then I realized that the sense of panic we felt was wholly unfounded. The reason there was light where Robert was standing, and darkness everywhere else in the room, was because his vision was clearer than ours. His clarity of vision was on a whole other level, a level the rest of the room had not yet attained. He had a clarity of vision that could not be achieved through study and knowledge, but only through a change in context. His context gave him a whole different perception of the things yet to come. It allowed him to not just see through the darkness but to sweep away the darkness, flooding his world with light. There was no darkness where he stood, because there was no darkness in his world.

That was the moment he gave me a truly great gift: a change of context. The clouds broke, the rain stopped, and the wind died. It was as if I had awakened from a bad dream. The gift Robert bestowed upon me was the revelation that the greatest opportunity in the history of mankind had just been laid at my feet. All I had to do was reach down and pick it up.

Knowledge is power. It is power that can be worn like a suit of armor. Truth can be a weapon. A weapon, which can be wielded like a sword, slicing through the propaganda and misinformation, laying them bare for all to see. Armed with these tools, I march headlong into the storm, not with fear, but with enthusiasm.

You are now armed with this knowledge, while 99 percent of the population remains in that comfortable bliss that ignorance provides, just going about their daily lives. This knowledge empowers you. You are now well in front of the herd.

I have often said that this period of time is like cresting the top of the highest peak of a roller coaster and staring down at the black void below. You can either be terrified, or sit in anxious anticipation of the thrills yet to come.

Well, one day soon, the general public will finally wake up and discover that they too are riding that roller coaster. Only they will not know where they are. They will be disoriented and confused, and sheer terror will grip them as they crest the top of the highest peak and glimpse, for the first time, the black void that will soon engulf them.

I have often said that this period of time is like cresting the top of the highest peak of a roller coaster and staring down at the black void below. You can either be terrified, or sit in anxious anticipation of the thrills yet to come.

One day soon, the general public will finally wake up and discover that they too are riding that roller coaster. Only they will not know where they are. They will be disoriented and confused, and sheer terror will grip them as they crest the top of the highest peak and glimpse, for the first time, the black void that will soon engulf them.

When the roller coaster reaches the bottom the public will have become desperate for precious metals, and in their panic they will rush to buy gold and silver. They will offer you their goods, services, and investments at fire-sale values. By selling your gold and silver when the public needs it the most, the full weight of the wealth transfer will have been completed, and you will have done very, very well.

Then with your new fortune of real estate, stocks, and other assets, you can ride the next big economic wave up. For now you know the formula. Everything runs in waves and cycles, and history just repeats and repeats.

Once again, the accounting has begun, and it will not stop until the full accounting is completed. Gold and silver have revalued themselves throughout the centuries and called on fiat paper to account for itself. In doing so, gold and silver bring fraudulent money to justice. They've always done this, and they always will.

It is as certain as the sunrise.

Resources

Educational Web Sites

RichDad.com
GoldSilver.com
Silver-Investor.com
FinancialSense.com
DollarCollapse.com
SilverStockReport.com
GATA.org
LemetropoleCafe.com
ShadowStats.com
NowAndFutures.com
Sharelynx.com
321gold.com
Gold-Eagle.com
TheBullAndBear.com
SilverStrategies.com
SilverBearCafe.com
GoldSeek.com

SilverSeek.com

PrudentBear.com

MarketOracle.com

Korelin Economic Report: kereport.com

Free Market News Network: fmnn.com

Jim Sinclair's MineSet: jsmineset.com

Ludwig von Mises Institute: mises.org

The Grandfather Economic Report: http://mwhodges.home.att.net/

Theodore Butler: ButlerResearch.com (look under free archives)

Sprott Asset Management: Sprott.com, (look under "market outlook")

Subscription Newsletters

Dow Theory Letters: DowTheoryLetters.com

The Morgan Report: Silver-Investor.com

Freemarket Gold & Money Report: fgmr.com

Casey Research: CaseyResearch.com

The Aden Forecast: AdenForecast.com

The Dines Letter: DinesLetter.com

Resource Opportunities: ResourceOpportunities.com

Jay Taylor's gold and technology Report: MiningStocks.com

Gold Mining Stock Report: GoldMiningStockReport.com

How to Be a Watchdog

U.S. Government Accountability Office: Gao.gov

U.S. Treasury: ustreas.gov

Federal Reserve: federalreserve.gov, Statistics: federalreserve.gov/releases

Federal Reserve system (all branches), federalreserveonline.org

Ron Paul: dailypaul.com; : house.gov/paul; ronpaul.org

Conventions

Cambridge House Recourse Investment Conferences:
CambridgeHouse.ca

IIC Resourse Investor Conferences: iiconf.com
The Money Show: MoneyShow.com
New Orleans Investment Conference: NewOrleansConference.com
The Silver Summit: TheSilverSummit.com

Other

CPM Group: cpmGroup.com
GFMS: gfms.co.uk
World Gold Council: Gold.org
Silver Institute: SilverInstitute.org

Suggested Reading

All of the books listed below were used as references and source
material for this book.

ABCs of Gold Investing, Michael J. Kosares
A History of Money from Ancient Times to the Present Day,
   Glyn Davies
A Monetary History of the United States, 1867–1960, Milton Friedman
   and Anna Jacobson Schwartz
America's Great Depression, Murray N. Rothbard
Big Fortunes in Gold and Silver, Howard Ruff
Buy Gold Now, Shayne McGuire
Buffettology, Mary Buffett and David Clark
The Case Against the Fed, Murray N. Rothbard
The Coming Economic Collapse, Stephen Leeb
The Coming Collapse of the Dollar, James Turk and John Rubino
The CPM Gold Yearbook 2008, CPM Group
The CPM Silver Yearbook 2008, CPM Group
Crash Proof, Peter Schiff
The Creature from Jekyll Island, G. Edward Griffin
The Dollar Crisis, Richard Duncan
The Economic Consequences of the Peace, by John Maynard Keynes

Empire of Debt, Bill Bonner and Addison Wiggin

Essays on the Great Depression, Ben S. Bernanke

Extraordinary Popular Delusions and the Madness of Crowds, Charles Mackey, 1841

Fiat Money Inflation in France, Andrew D. White

Financial Armageddon, Michael J. Pnazner

Financial Reckoning Day, William Bonner and Addison Wiggin

Get the Skinny on Silver Investing, David Morgan

The Great Bust Ahead, Dan Arnold

Manias, Panics and Crashes, Charles P. Kindelberger and Robert Aliber

Mobs, Messiahs and Markets, William Bonner, Lila Rajiva

Rich Dad's Increase Your Financial IQ, Robert T. Kiyosaki

Rich Dad's Prophecy, Robert T. Kiyosaki with Sharon L. Lechter

Rule by Secrecy, Jim Marrs

Secrets of the Federal Reserve, Eustact Mullins

Secrets of the Temple, William Greider

Silver Bonanza, James U. Blanchard III and Franklin Sanders

What Has Government Done to Our Money?, Murray N. Rothbard

About the Author

Mike Maloney has been a precious metals investor advisor to Robert Kiyosaki since 2005 and has spoken to audiences throughout the United States on the benefits of precious metals investing. A student of economics, Mike is regarded as an expert on economic cycles and capitalizing on the opportunities they afford.

As an entrepreneur, Mike has been involved in sales, manufacturing, and trade show production firms for over twenty years. And as an award-winning designer, Mike's revolutionary stereo designs are on display at the Royal Victoria and Albert Museum in London.

Since 2002, Mike has specialized in gold and silver investment education, and has had the privilege of interacting with influential government and economic leaders, such as Congressman and presidential candidate Ron Paul.

Mike is the owner and founder of GoldSilver.com, an online precious metals dealership that specializes in delivery of gold and silver to a customer's doorstep, arranges for special secured storage, or for placement in one's IRA account. Additionally, GoldSilver.com provides invaluable research and commentary for its clients, assisting them in their wealth-building endeavors.

Michael Maloney's GoldSilver.com is an education company and precious metals dealer.

We believe that gold and silver are the premier investments for the current financial cycle.

GoldSilver.com offers gold and silver:

Delivered to your door

•

Stored in a vault

•

In your IRA

Sign up for the free newsletter at:

www.goldsilver.com

Bestselling Books by
Robert T. Kiyosaki & Sharon L. Lechter

Rich Dad Poor Dad
What the Rich Teach Their Kids About Money
that the Poor and Middle Class Do Not

Rich Dad's CASHFLOW Quadrant
Rich Dad's Guide to Financial Freedom

Rich Dad's Guide to Investing
What the Rich Invest In that the Poor and Middle Class Do Not

Rich Dad's Rich Kid Smart Kid
Give Your Child a Financial Head Start

Rich Dad's Retire Young Retire Rich
How to Get Rich Quickly and Stay Rich Forever

Rich Dad's Prophecy
Why the Biggest Stock Market Crash in History is Still Coming...
And How You Can Prepare Yourself and Profit From it!

Rich Dad's Success Stories
Real-Life Success Stories from Real-Life People
Who Followed the Rich Dad Lessons

Rich Dad's Guide to Becoming Rich Without Cutting Up Your Credit Cards
Turn "Bad Debt" into "Good Debt"

Rich Dad's Who Took My Money?
Why Slow Investors Lose and Fast Money Wins!

Rich Dad Poor Dad for Teens
The Secrets About Money – That You Don't Learn In School!

Rich Dad's Escape from the Rat Race
How to Become a Rich Kid by Following Rich Dad's Advice

Rich Dad's Before You Quit Your Job
Ten Real-Life Lessons Every Entrepreneur Should Know
About Building a Multi-Million Dollar Business

Rich Dad's Increase Your Financial IQ
Get Smarter With Your Money
www.richdad.com

Bestselling Books by Rich Dad's Advisors

Sales Dogs
by Blair Singer
Reveal the Five Simple but Critical Revenue - Generating Skills

Own Your Own Corporation Updated and Revised 2008
by Garret Sutton
Don't Climb the Corporate Ladder, Why Not Own the Corporate Ladder?

How To Buy & Sell A Business
by Garrett Sutton
Strategies Used by Successful Entrepreneurs

The ABC's of Real Estate Investing
by Ken McElroy
Learn How To Acheive Wealth and Cash Flow Through Real Estate

The ABC's of Building A Business Team That Wins
by Blair Singer
How to Get Rich Quickly and Stay Rich Forever

The ABC's of Getting Out of Debt
by Garrett Sutton
Strategies for Overcoming Bad Debt, as Well as
Using Good Debt To Your Advantage

The ABC's of Writing Winning Business Plans
by Garrett Sutton
Learn to Focus Your Plan for the Business and Format Your plan to Impress
About Building a Multi-Million Dollar Business

The Advanced Guide to Real Estate Investing
by Ken McElroy
How to Identify the Hottest Markets and Secure the Best Deals

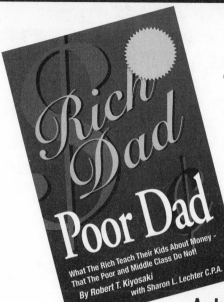

THE **BOOK** THAT **STARTED** IT **ALL**

**Are you ready
to change
the way you think
about money?**

An International Bestseller!

Learn how
to make your money
work for you!

Robert Kiyosaki
Investor, Entrepreneur,
Educator and Author

NEW from...
Robert Kiyosaki
*Rich Dad's Increase
Your Financial IQ*
Get Smarter with Your Money

For more information go to: www.richdad.com

The New York Times writes:

"Move over, Monopoly®...

A new board game that aims to teach people how to get rich is gaining fans the world over!"

WHY PLAY GAMES?

Play often and learn
what it takes to
get out of the Rat Race—
for good!

Games are **powerful learning tools** because they enable people to experience 'hands-on' learning. As a **true reflection of behavior,** games are a **window to our attitudes,** our **abilities to see opportunities,** and **assess risk and rewards.**

Each of the CASHFLOW® games creates a forum in which to evaluate life decisions regarding money and finances and immediately see the results of your decisions.

For more information go to: www.richdad.com

CASHFLOW Clubs

The Benefits of Joining
a CASHFLOW Club

Invest Time Before You Invest Money

The philosophy of The Rich Dad Company is that there are only two things you can invest: time and money. We recommend you invest some time studying and learning before you invest your money. The CASHFLOW games offer the opportunity to learn and 'invest' with 'play money' – before you invest real money.

Meet New Friends from Around the World

When you visit or join a CASHFLOW Club (or play the CASHFLOW games on line) you'll meet like-minded people – from all over the world. The world is filled with people with negative attitudes, know-it-all attitudes and loser attitudes. The type of person a CASHFLOW Club attracts is a person who is open minded, wants to learn and wants to develop his or her potential.

Have Fun Learning

Learning should be fun! Too often financial education is dull, boring and fear-based. Many financial experts want to educate you on how risky investing is and why you should trust them. That is not the Rich Dad philosophy on learning. We believe that learning should be fun and cooperative and lead you toward becoming smarter about money so you can tell the difference between good and bad financial advice.

Find a CASHFLOW Club near you:
www.richdad.com

Rich Dad's Wisdom:
The Power of Words

Words are gasoline for your brain. If you improve your financial vocabulary, you will become richer and richer. The good news is: words are free. Which proves, once more, that it does not take money to make money. To expand your vocabulary beyond the financial terms in the glossary you'll find on the Rich Dad web site you might consider acquiring a dictionary of financial terms. When you look up financial words on a regular basis (or look up the definition of a term you hear but do not understand) you may find yourself becoming richer and richer.

An example of the power of words: When people advise you to get out of debt, do they know what they are talking about?

> When you buy a bond, you are buying debt. For example, a U.S. T-bill is a bond – an IOU from the U.S. government. So when you buy a bond you are buying debt...debt that is an asset to you and a liability to the government. So debt can be good. Some of the richest people in the world (as well as financial institutions) get richer because they invest in debt.

When a banker says your house is an asset...ask yourself: Whose asset is it? By definition, assets put money in your pocket and liabilities take money from your pocket. When you look at your bank's financial statement, you can better see whose asset your home really is...

To improve your brain's financial power...improve your financial vocabulary. Words are fuel for your brain!

To learn more about...

Rich Dad's Coaching • Rich Dad's Franchise
Rich Dad's Education
Visit: www.richdad.com

Notes

Notes